Give Thanks and Praise

Children's Liturgies
and Celebrations for
Sundays, Weekdays,
and Saints Days

Give Thanks and Praise

Patricia Mathson

AVE MARIA PRESS
Notre Dame, Indiana 46556

Acknowledgments

© 1997 by Ave Maria Press, Inc.

International Standard Book Number: 0-87793-605-6

Cover design and text design by Katherine Robinson Coleman.

Idea for "Lenten trees" taken from "Fruitful Lenten Trees," by Sister Frances Chircho, *Catechist* (February 1985), p. 28.

Printed and bound in the United States of America.

*Dedicated to all children
everywhere.
May they know in their hearts
that God loves
each and every one
of them.
And may all catechists and parents
help them celebrate
each day
the joy and hope
of being God's children.*

Contents

February

March

April

May

Planning Liturgies with Children

The Mass is at the heart of our faith as Catholics. Through the Mass we worship our God together and celebrate all that God—Father, Son, and Holy Spirit—has done for us. At Mass we gather together as the people of God, listen to the word of God, celebrate Jesus in the eucharist, and then go forth to witness to Christ in our lives.

Children's liturgies help children grow in understanding that in our celebration of the liturgy we encounter Christ in the word and in the eucharist. The goal of these special liturgies is to lead children toward fuller participation in the celebration of the Sunday eucharist with the parish community.

These liturgies can be used for children in religious education programs or Catholic schools. This book is intended for presiders, school principals, directors of religious education, liturgy directors, parents, teachers, catechists, and all those who help children learn to celebrate God in their lives. In addition, the ideas can be adapted by parishes that have children's liturgy of the word and those with lectionary-based catechetical programs. Elements of these liturgies can be also used for prayer services at home, in weekday programs, and in Sunday classes.

Organization of Liturgies

The liturgies in this book are planned to celebrate all the seasons of the church year, for it is through the liturgical seasons that we walk with Jesus Christ and celebrate his birth, life, death, and resurrection. Specifically, the liturgies are arranged by month to follow the school year. Liturgies have been included for selected weekdays, Sundays, feast days, holy days, and saint's days. During the Triduum, however, children should not be separated from the assembly, but instead participate in parish liturgies with their families.

Mass Guidelines

The *Directory for Masses with Children* is an important resource when planning children's liturgies. This document, directed at Masses celebrated with elementary-age children, gives guidelines for those adaptations which, according to the *Directory*, may be made in planning liturgies with children. Adaptations are permitted to encourage children's participation and understanding; it is permissible, for example, to include only one reading in addition to the gospel in order to make the Mass simpler. The *Directory for Masses with Children* explains the elements of the Mass that must be included and the importance of planning liturgies with children. Most of the adaptations explored in this document are for Masses with children in which few adults participate.

Liturgical guidelines from other church documents should also be followed. For example, the Gloria may be used on Sundays, but is not used during Lent and Advent. This prayer can also be used on feasts and solemnities. The creed can be included on Sundays and solemnities; the Apostles' Creed may also be used.

Enrichment Ideas

Supplementary ideas and activities are suggested throughout this book to enhance children's worship and encourage the participation of the assembly in special ways. Ideas include posters, banners, processions, intention book, meditations, prayer cards, service projects, and others. These activities help foster understanding and involve the children more fully in the celebration of the Mass.

Scripture Readings

The liturgies with children in this book are based on scripture from all three cycles of Sunday readings as well as selected weekday readings. Gospel readings from all four gospels have been included so that children can hear the word of God proclaimed from each one.

Children should hear the word of God proclaimed in a manner they can understand. A translation of scripture should be used rather than a paraphrase, and the appropriate scripture readings for the particular day should be used unless there is a good reason.

The *Lectionary for Masses with Children* is a wonderful source for readings and psalms for children's liturgies. The readings have been shortened so they are easier for children to understand. This lectionary includes the three-year cycle of Sunday readings as well as readings for weekdays. Also included are readings for saint's-day liturgies with children. The liturgies planned throughout this book include reference numbers to the *Lectionary for Masses with Children* in order to easily find the appropriate scriptures.

Homilies

The homily should help children see the relationship of the scriptures to their lives. We want children to understand the importance of the word of God in the way they live. This book includes ideas for homilies which engage the interest of children in exploring the readings. Stories, props, questions, and other ideas are also suggested to involve the children in the homily.

General Intercessions

It is important for children to learn to pray for their own needs and the needs of others. Through the prayer of the faithful at Mass, we pray together as the people of God for the needs of all people. Suggested general intercessions are included for each liturgy based on the readings and the feast day being celebrated. These intercessions are given in language that children can understand and pray together.

Eucharistic Prayers

The eucharistic prayer—a prayer of thanksgiving to our God—is the high point and center of the liturgical celebration. Three special eucharistic prayers have been developed and approved for use in liturgies with children. The language is simpler and more suitable for children's worship and understanding.

Eucharistic Prayer I emphasizes giving thanks and praise to God. Eucharistic Prayer II tells of living as children of God and offers the most often sung acclamations as well as opportunities for student participation. Eucharistic Prayer III speaks of unity and features a seasonal insert for Easter. These eucharistic prayers are found in *The Sacramentary*.

Music

Music touches children's hearts and helps them praise God and therefore is an important part of all liturgical celebration. For children's liturgies, the music should be carefully chosen to fit the needs of children and the standards of good liturgy. It is important that music be suitable for children's voices and appropriate to their level of understanding.

Gestures help children learn the meaning of the songs and can also help them to understand parts of the Mass such as the Gloria and the creed. An adult can lead gestures from a place that does not block the view of the altar.

Children's hymnals are available that contain all the songs and service music needed for children's liturgies. If song books are not purchased, permission must be obtained to print lyrics. Most music publishers have both a one-time fee and a yearly fee.

The music chosen should reinforce the theme of the scripture readings assigned to that day and to the season of the church year. Music must also be selected to fit the parts of the Mass when it is sung: the song should not be longer or shorter than the action it accompanies.

- The *gathering song* should be lively and reflect the readings. This song should be appropriate to gather the children together as the people of God and should also reflect the liturgical season.

- The *responsorial psalm*, if sung, should be chosen from a children's hymnal or children's psalm book. The responsorial psalm is our response to the first reading from scripture.

- The *song during the presentation of the gifts* may speak of bread and wine or of serving others. It should be a song of praise and seasonal in nature. Instrumental music or a period of silence may be used instead.

- The *communion song* reflects this important rite which is the climax of our eucharistic celebration together. It should express our unity as we come to the table of the Lord and should be appropriate to the season of the liturgical year.

- The music of the *closing song* should send us forth to love God and love others. It should also reflect the season of the church year being celebrated.

Planning Form

A special planning form is included on pp. 189-190. This form has a place to list the songs, eucharistic prayer, and other parts of the Mass. Any part to be omitted should also be noted. The completed form should be duplicated and given to the presider, cantor, and the coordinator of children's participation.

Children's Roles

One of the wonderful benefits of liturgies with children is the opportunity for children to assume special roles within the liturgy. In these liturgies, children can have additional responsibility for ministry to other children. This increased participation encourages understanding and involvement in the Mass.

A child may carry in the cross at the beginning of Mass and out at the end of Mass. The children's lectionary may also be carried by a child. In some celebrations, additional items may be carried in the opening procession by children to enhance the environment or student understanding. The children's lectionary and any other items are carried in after the cross.

Children may act as readers to proclaim the first and second readings. The children need to be reminded to speak up loudly enough to be heard by everyone in the assembly. Children can also read the verses of the responsorial psalm, with a different child reading each stanza. Each child stands at the microphone until the responsorial is sung; then the next child comes forward to read. This curtails movement during the singing.

The general intercessions may be led by children, with each child reading one of the petitions. All the children who are reading an intention come forward at the same time. They step up to the microphone when it is their turn to read. Then after all the intercessions have been read, the children return to the assembly together. Sometimes children may want to help write the intercessions with the help of the teacher. The intercessions should reflect concerns in the parish, the community, and the world. A form for the general intercessions is included in the resource section in the back of this book.

In addition, children can act as gift-bearers, bringing forward the bread and wine during the presentation of the gifts. Donations for the poor or gifts for people in need may also be brought forward just before the bread and wine. Nothing else should be brought forward in this procession.

Children may also participate in a special reflection after communion. This meditation can help the children in the assembly understand the special feast or season being celebrated.

At Mass, children can also act as hospitality ministers. They can greet people as they arrive and leave. Children who are trained altar servers may also serve at Masses with children.

It is important to ask for volunteers so that children are comfortable with their roles. Children who have special roles should have the opportunity to practice during the week before the liturgy or in the time immediately before the liturgy begins. Notes should go home to the parents if a child has to come early to get special training. Copies of the readings and general intercessions should be sent home so that the children can practice with their parents, and extra copies of the intercessions should be available at the liturgy for those who leave them at home.

The *Directory for Masses with Children* encourages children's participation in liturgies in which the assembly is mostly children and few adults participate. This is an important document to consult when planning children's liturgies.

Participation Form

A form for planning children's participation is included at the back of this book. The form can be adapted by the person responsible for organizing special roles for children during each liturgy. A place is given to record each child's name next to the action for which they volunteered.

Role of the Assembly

It is important to remember and to stress that every baptized child and adult has an important role as a member of the assembly at each liturgy that we celebrate together. We are to lift up our hearts and voices together to our God and give praise. Children should be made aware of the importance of participating fully in the songs, responses, and prayers of the Mass.

Art and Environment

In planning art and environment for children's liturgies, it is important to follow liturgical guidelines and be mindful of the season during which a liturgy is celebrated. In many parishes, a children's liturgy will be celebrated in the church and thus the seasonal art and environment will already be in place.

Extras, such as a poster, can be added if appropriate for a particular liturgy. Remember that no flowers should be included for the environment during Lent, although it is permissible to place flowers in front of the statues of Mary and Joseph on their feast days even during the Lent season. During the Easter season the paschal candle should be lit for each liturgy.

Preparation

Children's liturgies require special planning by adults. The Mass coordinator must carefully set up the necessary vessels and supplies. The prayer leader who offers the greeting at the beginning of the Mass may need to be an adult so that he or she can welcome the children and get their attention that Mass is beginning. The cantor should also be an adult or older student. Someone must be available throughout the Mass to prompt the children when it is time to come forward for their parts. Enough adults, trained as eucharistic ministers for the cup and the bread, must be present.

Seating

Children should sit with their classmates and teachers. Younger and older siblings may be invited to these liturgies along with other family members. Seating should then be provided for families at the back of the church or worship space. It should be understood that everyone at these liturgies should be participating by singing the songs, saying the responses, and praying the prayers along with the children. We are all important members of the assembly.

Collection

It is not necessary to take up a collection at a children's liturgy. However, if other family members are attending and it is a Sunday or special feast day, collection baskets can be left on a table in the back of the worship space for the envelopes and cash. A second collection requires a separate marked basket. Be sure an adult is assigned to take the collection to the proper place as soon as Mass is over.

Liturgies in Places Other Than the Church

Sometimes, for a variety of reasons, children's liturgies must be held in a place other than the church such as a gym, cafeteria, or hall. In these cases, it is important to pay attention to art and environment to set a reverent tone for worship. Silk plants can be used to enhance the environment. These plants can be arranged in front of the ambo or altar. Also, mums can be added among the leaves for liturgies in the fall. Lilies can be used for Easter season liturgies.

The altar cloth can also reflect the season of the church year. For example, a green cloth can be used for ordinary time. Banners made of felt or other fabric can be used effectively in areas other than the church to remind the assembly of the day or season being celebrated. Posters made by the children can hang on the back wall.

Many items will need to be collected and brought to the place where the liturgy will be held. An altar or table is needed, plus a credence table, and a table for the gifts. An ambo with a microphone should also be provided from which to proclaim the word of God.

Items needed for Mass include a chalice, cups, patens, altar cloth, pitcher with water and bowl, unconsecrated hosts and wine, and a large host. The carafe of wine and the bowl of unconsecrated hosts should be placed on the gift table before the children's liturgy begins. Linens needed include an altar cloth, purificators, towel and pall. Candles and matches should also be provided. One special note is that any consecrated, but unconsumed, hosts must be taken to the tabernacle right after Mass by a eucharistic minister.

A sacramentary is needed for the presider and a children's lectionary for the readings. The proper place should be marked in each book before Mass begins. The presider may be asked to bring over his own vestments.

A music stand and microphone are needed for the cantor. A keyboard or guitar is desirable for music. Music books should be provided for all members of the assembly even if they have to share.

Chairs should be provided in separate areas for the presider, the altar servers and the choir members. Children can sit with their classes on the floor. Chairs should be provided for family members if they will be at Mass.

Liturgical Catechesis

Children's liturgies, like all Masses, are not to be times of instruction, but of worship. Children should be prepared during classes and at home to celebrate fully all that God has done for us by participating fully in the Mass.

At the end of each liturgy, we are sent forth to witness to all that Jesus Christ said and did. Hopefully, children's liturgies will help children live the message of Jesus Christ now and in the future.

Resources Needed

Below are two lists. The first lists of materials which are basic for planning and celebrating these liturgies. If they are not immediately available to you, check with your parish library or diocesan resource center. The second lists other resources which various liturgies mention. Substitutions can be made for these materials; you may find other music or stories which are equally appropriate.

Basic Resources

Book of Blessings. New York, NY: Catholic Book Publishing Co., 1989.

Lectionary for Masses with Children. New York, NY: Catholic Book Publishing Co., 1993. Also published by Liturgy Training Publications and by The Liturgical Press.

The Liturgy Documents: A Parish Resource. Chicago, IL: Liturgy Training Publications, 1991.

The Sacramentary. New York, New York: Catholic Book Publishing Company, 1985. Also published by The Liturgical Press.

The Sacramentary Supplement. New York, New York: Catholic Book Publishing Company, 1994.

Other Resources

God Made Us Different. (Helen Caswell) Nashville, TN: Abingdon Press, 1988.

Hymnal for Catholic Students. Chicago, IL: G.I.A. Publications, Inc. and Liturgy Training Publications, 1988.

The Lady of Guadalupe. (Tomie de Paola) New York, NY: Holiday House, 1980.

Rise Up and Sing: Young People's Music Resource. Portland, OR: OCP Publications, 1992.

Saints for All Season. (Sr. Mary Fearon, RSM) Brown ROA: 1992.

Sing for Joy: Psalm Settings for God's Children. Collegeville, MN: The Liturgical Press, 1992.

Sing Out! A Children's Psalter. Schiller Park, IL: World Library Publications, 1994.

What Is Faith? (Virginia Mueller) Cincinnati, OH: Standard Publishing Co., 1994.

Young People's Glory & Praise. (*Vol.1*, 1984 and *Vol. 2*, 1991) Phoenix, AZ: North American Liturgy Resources, 1984. Now available through OCP Publications.

SEPTEMBER

SERVICE TO OTHERS
WEEKDAY IN ORDINARY TIME

Welcome:

Welcome to all of you. The gospel today calls us to help people as Jesus showed us. We are to serve others as Jesus was the servant of all. Care cards made by some of the children will be brought forward in the entrance procession as a sign of caring about others. (See end of liturgy for information on care cards.)

Introductory Rites

Gathering Song:

Let us stand and sing out together our gathering song "Reach Out." (Carey Landry, *Young People's Glory and Praise*, OCP.)

Entrance Procession:

Three children accompany the presider, carrying in the cross, children's lectionary, and a basket of care cards as the gathering song is sung.

 Cross   Basket of care cards   Children's lectionary

Liturgy of the Word

First Reading:

(This reading tells us that faith must lead to good deeds.)
Three children read the letter of James 2:14-18 from the Lectionary for Masses with Children #217.

  A reading from the letter of James . . .
Can that kind of faith save you?

  If you know . . . is all alone and dead!

  Suppose someone disagrees . . . The word of the Lord.

Responsorial Psalm:

"Praise the Lord, My Soul." (Carey Landry, *Young People's Glory and Praise,* OCP.)

Two children read Psalm 146:6-9 from the Lectionary for Masses with Children #217.

  God always . . . food to the hungry.

 The LORD . . . looks after strangers.

Gospel Acclamation:

"Alleluia." (Jack Miffleton, *Young People's Glory and Praise,* OCP.)

Gospel:

(This gospel tells us to do good to those who cannot pay us back.)
Presider proclaims Luke 14:12-14 from the Lectionary for Masses with Children #217.
A reading from the holy gospel according to Luke . . .

Homily Ideas:

Jesus calls us to help others who cannot or will not be able to repay us. We are to love as Jesus did without conditions. All people are called to God's kingdom. We are to help the poor and forgotten in our local community and support projects that benefit those in need around the world. We should also get other people involved. We must have the courage to put our faith into action and do what is right.

General Intercessions:

The prayers are read by five children, with the assembly responding.

 To our petitions please respond: "Lord, hear our prayer." May we live as witnesses to God's love each day, we pray to the Lord . . .

 May we reach out to the poor and those in need, we pray to the Lord . . .

 May people everywhere learn to share with others in the name of Jesus, we pray to the Lord . . .

 May we learn to treat all people with dignity and respect, we pray to the Lord . . .

May we see Jesus Christ in everyone we meet, we pray to the Lord . . .

Liturgy of the Eucharist

Presentation Song:

The song during the presentation of the gifts today is "Jesus, Jesus." (Carey Landry, *Young People's Glory and Praise*, OCP.)

Presentation of the Gifts:

As the song is sung, two children carry the gifts of bread and wine to the altar and hand them to the presider.

 Wine   Bread

Eucharistic Prayer:

Eucharistic Prayer for Masses with Children II.

Eucharistic Acclamations:

"Acclamations for Prayer II." (Carey Landry, *Young People's Glory and Praise*, OCP.)

Communion Song:

As we come forward to share the eucharist, let us sing "Come to My Heart." (Joe Pinson, *Young People's Glory and Praise*, OCP.)

Concluding Rite

Closing Song:

We leave today to go and do God's will. Let's sing together our closing song, "Service." (Buddy Ceasar, *Young People's Glory and Praise*, OCP.)

Closing Procession:

The children who carried in the cross and children's lectionary now carry them out, accompanying the presider, as the closing song is sung.

 Cross   Children's lectionary

Care Cards

All of us are called to care about other people in the name of Jesus Christ. Children can be encouraged to think about what they can do for others by filling out "care cards."

Talk in class about how we should reach out to others as Jesus teaches us. Discuss with the children specific ways to show caring for other people.

Ask the children to fill out individual care cards stating: "I will show care to others as Jesus teaches us by _____." (See p.193 for a reproducible care card form.) Children write in what they will do for other people and sign their names. Cards may be decorated with crayons, markers, or heart stickers.

Each child adds a completed care card to a basket. This basket is carried in the entrance procession at the children's liturgy and placed in front of the processional cross as a sign of caring about others in Jesus' name.

This idea personalizes the lesson for the students and helps them understand that we are to live what we believe.

THE FORGIVING FATHER
24TH SUNDAY IN ORDINARY TIME (C)

Welcome:

As we come together today, we remember that our God is a merciful and forgiving Father to us all. God loves us with an unending love. God will always forgive us.

Introductory Rites

Gathering Song:

Our gathering song is "Children of the Lord." (Carey Landry, *Young People's Glory and Praise*, OCP.)

Entrance Procession:

Two children accompany the presider, carrying in the cross and children's lectionary as the gathering song is sung.

 Cross   Children's lectionary

Penitential Rite:

(Children can help write the penitential rite for this Mass. See information at end of liturgy.)

We now ask the Father to forgive us, saying "Lord have mercy."
For the times we did not help other people,
    Lord, have mercy.
For the times we lied or were dishonest,
    Christ, have mercy.
For the times we did not respect the rights of others,
    Lord, have mercy.

Liturgy of the Word

First Reading:

(In this reading Paul tells how Christ has blessed his life.)

Child reads 1 Timothy:12-15b from the Lectionary for Masses with Children #127.

 A reading from the first letter of Paul to Timothy . . .

Responsorial Psalm:

"Protect Me, O God." (Julie Howard, *Sing for Joy*, LP.)

Gospel Acclamation:

"Alleluia." (Jack Miffleton, *Young People's Glory and Praise*, OCP.)

Gospel:

(This is the beautiful story of the forgiving father.)

Presider reads Luke 15:11-32 from the Lectionary for Masses with Children #127.

A reading from the holy gospel according to Luke . . .

Homily Ideas:

The gospel today we call the story of the forgiving Father. Why do you think this is so? (The father forgives the son.) God is like the Father in this story. God is always there to forgive us when we are sorry. The Father comes out to meet us and welcomes us back.

We must tell God we are sorry when we have done wrong. We must also tell the person we have hurt that we're sorry. Is it easy to say I'm sorry? (No.) It is difficult to ask forgiveness and admit that we have chosen to do something wrong.

Also we must make up for any harm we have caused. How can we do this? (*Get children's ideas.*) If we have lied, we must tell the truth. If we have stolen something, we must give it back. If we have been unkind to someone, we must be nice to them.

Creed:

Let's sing "We Believe," a song about our faith in God. (Carey Landry, *Young People's Glory and Praise*, OCP.)

General Intercessions:

The prayers are read by five children, with the assembly responding.

 Today we ask God's forgiveness for things we have done wrong. To our petitions please respond: "Lord, hear our prayer." We ask forgiveness for the times we have not followed your word in our lives. We pray to the Lord . . .

We ask forgiveness for the times we have not taken time to pray. We pray to the Lord . . .

 We ask forgiveness for the times we have not told the truth. We pray to the Lord . . .

 We ask forgiveness for the times when we have hurt others by our words or actions. We pray to the Lord . . .

 We ask forgiveness for the times we have not reached out to people in need. We pray to the Lord . . .

Liturgy of the Eucharist

Presentation Song:

As the table is prepared, we bring forward our gifts and sing "Peace Time." (Carey Landry, *Young People's Glory and Praise*, OCP.)

Presentation of the Gifts:

As the song is sung, two children carry the gifts of bread and wine to the altar and hand them to the presider.

 Wine   Bread

Eucharistic Prayer:

Eucharistic Prayer for Masses with Children II.

Eucharistic Acclamations:

"Acclamations for Eucharistic Prayer II." (Carey Landry, *Young People's Glory and Praise*, OCP.)

Lamb of God:

"Lamb of God." (Carey Landry, *Young People's Glory and Praise*, OCP.)

Communion Song:

Our song during Communion today is "God Is So Good." (Carey Landry, *Young People's Glory and Praise*, OCP.

Concluding Rite

Closing Song:

Our song as we leave today is "Glory and Praise to Our God." (Dan Schutte, S.J., *Young People's Glory and Praise*, OCP.)

Closing Procession:

The children who carried in the cross and children's lectionary now carry them out, accompanying the presider, as the closing song is sung.

 Cross   Children's lectionary

Penitential Rite

Students can help compose the prayers for the penitential rite at the children's liturgy. The week before the Mass, discuss the concept of asking forgiveness from God for our sins as the son did in the gospel of the forgiving father. Explain that one way to do this is during the penitential rite at Mass. Let the children know that God always hears our prayers and is ready to forgive us.

Discuss our responses during the penitential rite. To the first prayer we respond: "Lord, have mercy." To the second prayer our response is: "Christ, have mercy." To the third prayer we respond again: "Lord, have mercy." Explain that we ask God to forgive us not because we deserve it, but because our God is a merciful and loving Father.

Ask the students to think of some things we do for which we should be sorry and ask for God's forgiveness. These are actions that cause us to separate ourselves from God and from one another.

Write the ideas on the board. Then work with the students on combining the suggestions into three prayers. Write down the prayers for the presider to read at the penitential rite of the children's liturgy.

THE KINGDOM OF GOD
WEEKDAY IN ORDINARY TIME

Welcome:

Welcome to our liturgy. We remember that we are to work to bring about the kingdom of God in our world for all people. God's reign is present where we share with one another in Jesus' name.

Introductory Rites

Gathering Song:

Let us join in singing together our gathering song, "We Are the Church." (Christopher Walker, *Rise Up and Sing*, OCP.)

Entrance Procession:

Two children accompany the presider, carrying in the cross and children's lectionary as the gathering song is sung.

 Cross   Children's lectionary

Liturgy of the Word

First Reading:

(In this reading, Paul prays that Christ will live in our hearts.)
    Ephesians 3:16-17, 20-21 is read by two children from the Lectionary for Masses with Children #231.

 A reading from the letter of Paul to the Ephesians . . . deeply rooted in his love.

 I pray . . . The word of the Lord.

Responsorial Psalm:

"A New Song." (Julie Howard, *Sing for Joy*, LP.)

Gospel Acclamation:

"Alleluia, Shout with Joy." (Barbara Bridge and Dominic MacAller, *Rise Up and Sing*, OCP.)

Gospel:

(In this reading from Luke 17:20-21 we are reminded that God's kingdom is here with us.)

Presider reads from the Lectionary for Masses with Children #231. **A reading from the holy gospel according to Luke . . .**

Homily Ideas:

We are called to be signs of the kingdom of God in the world. We are to make a commitment to live as Jesus showed us. We are to reach out to all people. We are to live as people of peace, justice, and love in the name of Jesus Christ. We must pray, go to Mass, forgive others, and give to the poor. In this way, we live as people of the kingdom.

General Intercessions:

The prayers are read by five children, with the assembly responding.

 To our petitions please respond: "Lord, hear our prayer." May we be people of peace and justice in our lives, we pray to the Lord . . .

 May our church be a sign of Jesus' presence in the world, we pray to the Lord . . .

 May we be welcoming to those who are new to our parish, we pray to the Lord . . .

 May we praise God at all times for sending Jesus to us, we pray to the Lord . . .

 May we live as people of the kingdom in all we say and do, we pray to the Lord . . .

Liturgy of the Eucharist

Presentation Song:

As our gifts are brought forward, we will sing together "Spirit of Our God."
(Felicia Sandler and Barbara Bridge, *Rise Up and Sing*, OCP.)

Presentation of the Gifts:

As the song is sung, two children carry the gifts of bread and wine to the altar and hand them to the presider.

 Wine   Bread

Eucharistic Prayer and Acclamations:

"Eucharistic Prayer for Masses with Children II." (Christopher Walker, *Rise Up and Sing*, OCP.)

Communion Song:

As we come forward to the table of the Lord, we sing together "You Are My Hope." (Marie-Jo Thum, *Rise Up and Sing*, OCP.)

Communion Meditation:

Some of the children will now share with us a reflection on the meaning of living as people of the kingdom of God in our lives.
   Seven children come forward with letters spelling K-I-N-G-D-O-M to offer the "Kingdom Meditation." (See end of liturgy for instructions.)

Concluding Rite

Closing Song:

As we leave today to live as people of the kingdom, we sing "Welcome to the Kingdom." (G.W. Hardin and Barbara Bridge, *Rise Up and Sing*, OCP.)

Closing Procession:

The children who carried in the cross and children's lectionary now carry them out, accompanying the presider, as the closing song is sung.

 Cross   Children's lectionary

Kingdom Meditation

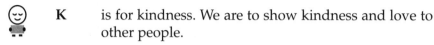

After communion, seven of the children can come forward for a meditation. The prayer leader leads into the meditation which is a reflection on the meaning of living as people of the kingdom of God.

The seven children each hold a letter on a card spelling out K-I-N-G-D-O-M. The children read a brief reflection off the back of the card one at a time as follows:

K is for kindness. We are to show kindness and love to other people.

I is for inspire. We are to inspire hope in the lives of others.

N is for needs. We are to pray for our needs and the needs of all people.

G is for God. We are to put God first in our lives.

D is for dare. We are to dare to live as people of peace and justice in the world.

O is for open. We are to be open to the Holy Spirit at work in our lives.

M is for mission. We share in the mission of Jesus Christ to tell the good news to all people.

To assure visibility for both the congregation and the young reader, each card should be at least 12" x 12", with each letter being at least 9" tall. The lettering for the reflection on the back of each card should be printed so as to facilitate ease of reading.

THE SAINT WHO CARED
SAINT VINCENT DE PAUL (SEPTEMBER 27)

Welcome:

We gather to remember Saint Vincent de Paul. He was a saint who helped the poor and the sick. Saint Vincent started several hospitals and encouraged others to reach out to people in need. He gave whatever he had to anyone who needed his help. Saint Vincent cared for all people as Jesus taught us to do.

Introductory Rites

Gathering Song:

We come together as a community of God's people and sing our gathering song, "Spirit of God, Come to Us." (Sr. Veronica McGrath and Carey Landry, *Young People's Glory and Praise, Volume Two*, OCP.)

Entrance Procession:

Two children accompany the presider, carrying in the cross and children's lectionary as the gathering song is sung.

 Cross   Children's lectionary

Liturgy of the Word

First Reading:

(This reading tells us that we show our love for others by helping them.)
    1 John 3:16-18 is read by a child from the Lectionary for Masses with Children #470, no. 6.

    A reading from the first letter of John . . .

Responsorial Psalm:

"Taste and See." (Carey Landry, *Young People's Glory and Praise, Volume Two*, OCP.)
Psalm 34:1-2,3-4,8-9 is read by children from the Lectionary for Masses with Children #471, no. 1.

 I will . . . and be glad.

 Honor the LORD . . . all my fears.

 Discover . . . ever be in need.

Gospel Acclamation:

"Alleluia." (Roc O'Connor, S.J., *Young People's Glory and Praise, Volume Two*, OCP.)

Gospel:

(This gospel teaches us the works of mercy.)
Presider proclaims Matthew 25:31-40 from the Lectionary for Masses with Children #473, no. 2.
A reading from the holy gospel according to Matthew . . .

Homily Ideas:

Saint Vincent de Paul worked among people in need in the rural areas of France. He gave them food, clothing, and love.
How can we live the works of mercy? (Give canned goods to a food pantry, raise money for a homeless shelter.)
We should also pray for the needs of other people as Jesus taught us.

General Intercessions:

The prayers are read by five children, with the assembly responding.

 We pray today for the needs of others. To our petitions, please respond: "Lord, hear our prayer." For homeless people: may they find shelter in the cold months ahead, we pray to the Lord . . .

 For those who are new in our schools and our community: may we welcome them in Jesus' name, we pray to the Lord . . .

 For people who are hungry: may the resources of the earth be used wisely to provide food for all people, we pray to the Lord . . .

For the sick: may they find comfort in knowing that God cares, we pray to the Lord . . .

 For all people in need: may we find a way to help them by sharing what we have, we pray to the Lord . . .

Liturgy of the Eucharist

Presentation Song:

Today, along with the bread and wine, the children will bring forward some of the books they have collected for children at the local homeless shelter. (See description of this project at end of liturgy.)

Our song during the presentation of the gifts is "Here Am I, O Lord." (Carey Landry, *Young People's Glory and Praise, Volume Two*, OCP.)

Presentation of the Gifts:

As the song is sung, three children carry the bread, wine, and the basket of books to the altar. The bread and wine are handed to the presider, and the basket of books is placed at the base of the processional cross.

 Basket of books   Wine   Bread

Eucharistic Prayer:

Eucharistic Prayer for Masses with Children II.

Eucharistic Acclamations:

(Roc O'Connor, S.J., and Elizabeth Staehler, *Young People's Glory and Praise, Volume Two*, OCP.)

Communion Song:

As we come forward for communion, we will sing together "At the Table of Jesus." (Carey Landry, *Young People's Glory and Praise, Volume Two*, OCP.)

Concluding Rite

Closing Song:

We have celebrated together; now let us go to live as Jesus taught us. Our closing song is "God Has Made Us a Family." (Carey Landry, *Young People's Glory and Praise, Volume Two,* OCP.)

Closing Procession:

The children who carried in the cross and children's lectionary now carry them out, accompanying the presider, as the closing song is sung.

 Cross   Children's lectionary

Book Collection

Saint Vincent de Paul worked with people who were poor and in need. Today in our own communities, some families have no place to stay. Many homeless shelters now have a sizeable population of families with children.

A great idea that benefits homeless children in the spirit of Saint Vincent de Paul is a children's book collection. The books become part of the children's library at the shelter. This project helps brighten the lives of homeless children.

Send home notes about this project at least a week before the feast of Saint Vincent de Paul, asking that children bring in new or good-condition used books. Explain the need for the project and which shelter will receive the books. (The reproducible letter on p. 194 can be duplicated and sent home to families.)

On the day of the liturgy, provide marked collection boxes in the back of the church. Some of the books should also be carried in a large basket in front of the bread and wine at the presentation of the gifts. The basket is placed at the foot of the processional cross.

After Mass, see that the books are brought to the shelter for children. This collection should be part of our ongoing Christian commitment to help the poor.

OCTOBER

PRAISE OUR CREATOR
SAINT FRANCIS OF ASSISI (OCTOBER 4)

Welcome:

We gather together to honor Saint Francis of Assisi. He was a saint who praised God for all of creation. Saint Francis saw the beauty in everything God made and in all people. Saint Francis told people that we are all brothers and sisters in Christ. He was a person of great compassion for others.

Introductory Rites

Gathering Song:

Let us stand and sing out with joy to God our Creator. Our gathering song today is "Canticle of the Sun" (Marty Haugen, *Rise Up and Sing*, OCP).

Entrance Procession:

Two children accompany the presider, carrying in the cross and children's lectionary as the gathering song is sung.

 Cross   Children's lectionary

Liturgy of the Word

First Reading:

(This reading tells how the followers of Jesus shared everything they had with each other.)

Acts 4:32-35 is read by two children from the Lectionary for Masses with Children #470, no. 1.

 A reading from the Acts of the Apostles . . . now alive.

 God greatly blessed . . . The word of the Lord.

Responsorial Psalm:

"Taste and See the Goodness of the Lord" (Alan J. Hommerding, *Sing Out*, WLP.)

Three children read Psalm 34:1-2, 3-4, 8-9 from the Lectionary for Masses with Children #471, no. 1.

 I will . . . be glad.

 Honor the LORD . . . from all my fears.

 Discover . . . ever be in need.

Gospel Acclamation:

"Alleluia, Shout with Joy." (Barbara Bridge and Dominic MacAller, *Rise Up and Sing,* OCP).

Gospel:

(In this gospel Jesus tells his disciples to give money to the poor.)

The presider reads Luke 12:32-34 from the Lectionary for Masses with Children #473, no. 4.

A reading from the holy gospel according to Luke . . .

Homily Ideas:

Saint Francis loved all of God's creation. What are some things that Francis loved? (Sun, moon, stars, birds, animals, people.) **Saint Francis is the patron saint of ecologists. What are some things we can do to help take care of creation?** (Conserve water resources, fight pollution, recycle things we use, work to save the rain forests.)

This is a San Damiano cross. *(Show the cross.)* **This is a copy of the cross from the church where Francis heard God's call in his life. He gave up a life of wealth for one of poverty. He gave away all that he had to the poor. This saint shared faith, hope, and love with others. How can we be like Saint Francis?** (Help other people, be joyful, act as peacemakers, forgive others, give to those in need.)

General Intercessions:

The prayers are read by six children, with the assembly responding.

 Our intercessions today are based on the beautiful prayer of Saint Francis. To each petition please respond: "Lord, hear our prayer." Where there is hatred, let us bring love, we pray to the Lord . . .

 Where there is injury, let us bring pardon, we pray to the Lord . . .

 Where there is doubt, let us bring faith, we pray to the Lord . . .

Where there is despair, let us bring hope, we pray to the Lord . . .

 Where there is darkness, let us bring light, we pray to the Lord . . .

 Where there is sadness, let us bring joy, we pray to the Lord . . .

Liturgy of the Eucharist

Presentation Song:

Join in our song during the presentation of the gifts, "Each Time That You Love." *(Barbara Bridge, Rise Up and Sing, OCP).*

Presentation of the Gifts:

As the song is sung, two children carry the gifts of bread and wine to the altar and hand them to the presider.

 Wine   Bread

Eucharistic Prayer:

Eucharistic Prayer for Masses with Children I.

Eucharistic Acclamations:

"Mass of Joy." (Marie-Jo Thum, *Rise Up and Sing*, OCP.)

Communion Song:

As we come together to the table of the Lord, let us sing "I, the Lord." (Owen Alstott, *Rise Up and Sing*, OCP.)

Concluding Rite

Announcement:

We will have the blessing of animals for the feast of Saint Francis in the courtyard immediately following Mass today. (See information at end of liturgy.)

Closing Song:

We go forth today singing "Take the Word of God with You." (James Harrison and Christopher Walker, *Rise Up and Sing*, OCP.)

Closing Procession:

The children who carried in the cross and children's lectionary now carry them out, accompanying the presider, as the closing song is sung.

 Cross   Children's lectionary

Blessing of Animals

A tradition for the feast of Saint Francis is the blessing of animals. Saint Francis loved all animals, and the story is told that he even preached to animals in the forest.

Notes should go home well in advance of the children's liturgy inviting parents to bring family pets to a designated outside area after Mass. Many different animals can be brought for the blessing including dogs, cats, hamsters, horses, turtles, hermit crabs, and others.

Immediately after the children's liturgy concludes, the children go outside and locate the waiting parents and pets. All the children are invited to the blessing. Even those children who do not have pets like to see the animals.

The order for the blessing of animals is found in the *Book of Blessings*. The priest invokes God's blessing on the animals. Then the intercessions are prayed. The priest says the prayer of blessing and uses holy water. A reading of the story of creation from Genesis is also included.

This is a very memorable way to celebrate the feast of Saint Francis.

MAKE YOUR LIGHT SHINE
WEEKDAY IN ORDINARY TIME

Welcome:

Welcome to our liturgy. Today we recall that we are to lead others to God by the way we live. We must make the light of Jesus Christ shine in our lives each day.

Introductory Rites

Gathering Song:

We gather together as the people of God and sing "Bring Forth the Kingdom." (Marty Haugen, *Hymnal for Catholic Students*, GIA.)

Entrance Procession:

Two children accompany the presider, carrying in the cross and children's lectionary as the gathering song is sung.

 Cross   Children's lectionary

Liturgy of the Word

First Reading:

(In this reading we are told that we are people of the light.)
   Two children read Ephesians 5:8-10 from the Lectionary for Masses with Children #193.)

 A reading from the letter of Paul . . . you belong to the Lord.

 So act like people . . . The word of the Lord.

Responsorial Psalm:

"The Lord Is My Light and My Salvation." (David Haas, *Hymnal for Catholic Students*, GIA.)

Psalm 27:1, 13-14 is read by two children from the Lectionary for Masses with Children #193.

 You, Lord . . . and I have no fears.

 I know . . . trust the Lord!

Gospel Acclamation:

"Alleluia: Form B." (Marty Haugen, *Hymnal for Catholic Students,* GIA.)

Gospel:

(This gospel calls us to make our light shine.)

Matthew 5:14-16 is read by presider from the Lectionary for Masses with Children #193.

A reading from the holy gospel according to Matthew . . .

Homily Ideas:

Jesus wants us to tell other people about God. When we do good actions, we let others see the light of Jesus in our lives. What are some good things we can do to let our light shine? (Go to Mass; tell others about God's love; help people who are poor.) **In these ways other people will learn about God's love through us. This coming week, try to do at least one good thing to let the light of your love shine.**

General Intercessions:

The prayers are read by five children, with the assembly responding.

 To our petitions please respond: "Lord, hear our prayer." May we always follow the light of Christ in our lives, we pray to the Lord . . .

 May others come to know God by our love for all people, we pray to the Lord . . .

 May we have the courage to do what is right even when it is difficult, we pray to the Lord . . .

 May our church always be a source of comfort and healing to people in times of trouble, we pray to the Lord . . .

 May we work for peace and thus bring hope to our world, we pray to the Lord . . .

Liturgy of the Eucharist

Presentation Song:

Join in our song during the presentation of the gifts, "Lord, You Give the Great Commission." *(Hymnal for Catholic Students, GIA.)*

Presentation of the Gifts:

As the song is sung, two children carry the gifts of bread and wine to the altar and hand them to the presider.

 Wine   Bread

Eucharistic Prayer:

Eucharistic Prayer for Masses with Children II.

Eucharistic Acclamations:

"Mass of Creation." (Marty Haugen, *Hymnal for Catholic Students,* GIA.)

Communion Song:

As we come forward to the table of the Lord, we sing together "Gift of Finest Wheat." *(Hymnal for Catholic Students, GIA.)*

Communion Meditation:

Some of the children will now come forward to share with us a reflection on making our light shine. Please join in the refrain. (See script at end of liturgy.)

Concluding Rite

Closing Song:

We go forth today singing "I Want to Walk as a Child of Light." *(Kathleen Thomerson, Hymnal for Catholic Students, GIA.)*

Closing Procession:

The children who carried in the cross and children's lectionary now carry them out, accompanying the presider, as the closing song is sung.

 Cross   Children's lectionary

Light Meditation

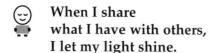

A reflection shared by one class of children after Communion can help all the students better understand what it means to make your light shine as we hear proclaimed in the gospel at this liturgy.

    The following reflections are read by individual children, one at a time, from the lectern. In between each reflection, all the children assembled for the liturgy are led in singing the verse to "This Little Light of Mine" *(Hymnal for Catholic Students, GIA)* by the cantor.

**When I share
what I have with others,
I let my light shine.**

**When I invite someone
to Mass with me on Sunday,
I let my light shine.**

**When I do what is right,
even when it is hard,
I let my light shine.**

**When I help people
who are in need,
I let my light shine.**

**When I respect
the rights of others,
I let my light shine.**

JESUS LOVES CHILDREN
27TH SUNDAY IN ORDINARY TIME (B)

Welcome:

We come together to celebrate that Jesus' love and care for each and every child. Each child is special. Jesus came for all people and cares about each one of us.

Introductory Rites

Gathering Song:

Let us begin our celebration by singing **"Children of God."** *(Christopher Walker, Rise Up and Sing, OCP.)*

Entrance Procession:

Two children accompany the presider, carrying in the Cross and children's lectionary as the gathering song is sung.

 Cross   Children's lectionary

Glory to God:

"Glory to God." (Michael Lynch, *Rise Up and Sing*, OCP.)

Liturgy of the Word

First Reading:

(In this reading we hear the story of the creation of man and woman.)

Genesis 2:18-24 is read by three children from the Lectionary for Masses with Children #135.

  A reading from the book of Genesis . . . got their names.

  Not one . . . out of the rib.

  The Lord God brought . . . The word of the Lord.

Responsorial Psalm:

"A New Song." (Julie Howard, *Sing for Joy*, LP.)

Gospel Acclamation:

"Alleluia, Shout with Joy." (Barbara Bridge and Dominic MacAller, *Rise Up and Sing*, OCP.)

Gospel:

(This gospel is the story of Jesus and the children.)
   The presider reads Mark 10:13-16 from the Lectionary for Masses with Children #135.

A reading from the holy gospel according to Mark . . .

Homily Ideas:

The presider may choose to ask the children to come forward if the assembly is small. The presider can then sit with the children on the altar steps during the homily.
   What happened in today's gospel reading? Review the story with the children. This gospel reminds us that Jesus loves each and every child very much. We can always turn to Jesus when we are happy or sad or afraid. Jesus is always with us. God makes each child special. I would like to share with you today a book called *God Makes Us Different.* **Read this book by Helen Caswell. (See the "Resources Needed" section on p. 16.)**
   Remember that each of us is special to God and loved by God. We should respect all people because God made all children everywhere.

Creed:

"We Believe." (Christopher Walker, *Rise Up and Sing*, OCP.)

General Intercessions:

The prayers are read by five children, with the assembly responding. (Children can write the general intercessions. See information at end of liturgy.)

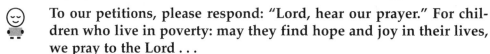

To our petitions, please respond: "Lord, hear our prayer." For children who live in poverty: may they find hope and joy in their lives, we pray to the Lord . . .

For children who find school work difficult: may they get the help they need, we pray to the Lord . . .

For children who are new or lonely: may other children reach out to them, we pray to the Lord . . .

For children in crisis situations: may they have the support of family and friends, we pray to the Lord . . .

 For children everywhere: may they realize that each of us is a special creation of God, who loves us with an unending love, we pray to the Lord . . .

Liturgy of the Eucharist

Presentation Song:

As the gifts of bread and wine are brought forward, join in singing "A Gift from Your Children." (Nancy Bourassa and Carey Landry, *Rise Up and Sing*, OCP.)

Presentation of the Gifts:

As the song is sung, two children carry the gifts of bread and wine to the altar and hand them to the presider.

 Wine   Bread

Eucharistic Prayer:

Eucharistic Prayer for Masses with Children I.

Eucharistic Acclamations:

"Mass of Joy." (Marie-Jo Thum, *Rise Up and Sing*, OCP.)

Communion Song:

Our song during Communion is "Jesus, You Are Bread for Us." (Christopher Walker, *Rise Up and Sing*, OCP.)

Concluding Rite

Solemn Blessing:

Blessing for Ordinary Time V. ("Solemn Blessings" section of *The Sacramentary.)*

47   *October*

Closing Song:

We go forth as children of God singing "We Are the Church." (Christopher Walker, *Rise Up and Sing,* OCP.)

Closing Procession:

The children who carried in the cross and children's lectionary now carry them out, accompanying the presider, as the closing song is sung.

 Cross   Children's lectionary

General Intercessions

Children can be encouraged to write their own general intercessions for children's liturgies. This is especially appropriate at the liturgy during which the story of Jesus and the children is proclaimed. Begin by reading this gospel with the children and discussing how Jesus loves all children.

Remind the children that we are to pray for other people. Talk about some of the needs of children around the world. Then lead the children in composing several general intercessions for children who need our prayers. Use the chalkboard to list the children's suggestions.

Five is a good number of intercessions for a children's liturgy. Combine some ideas and eliminate ones that are too similar. Each intention should end with "We pray to the Lord. . . ." This invites the assembly's response of "Lord, hear our prayer."

Write down the intercessions on paper. (A reproducible form for writing these prayers can be found on p. 192.) Ask for a volunteer to read each of the petitions at the children's liturgy.

This process helps the children to understand that we are to pray at Mass for the needs of others in our community and our world. These prayers are prayed from the heart because the children have been involved in composing them.

CALLED TO PEACE
WEEKDAY IN ORDINARY TIME

Welcome:

The readings remind us that we are called to be people of peace. Jesus Christ calls us to respect all people. We are to work for peace in our lives and in our world. Some of the children have written prayers for peace which will be carried in the entrance procession. (See instructions for "peace prayers" at end of liturgy.)

Introductory Rites

Gathering Song:

Let us stand now and sing out together our gathering song "Let There Be Peace on Earth." (Sy Miller and Jill Jackson, *Young People's Glory and Praise*, OCP.)

Entrance Procession:

Three children accompany the presider, carrying in the cross, children's lectionary, and box of peace prayers as the gathering song is sung.

 Cross   Box of peace prayers   Children's lectionary

Penitential Rite:

We now express our sorrow for the times when we did not live as people of peace. Let us pray together, saying "Lord, have mercy."

For the times when we were unkind to others,
    Lord, have mercy.
For the times when we lied or did not tell the truth,
    Christ, have mercy.
For the times when we argued over unimportant things,
    Lord, have mercy.

Liturgy of the Word

First Reading:

(In this reading Paul tells his followers that we were chosen to live together in peace.)

Two children read Colossians 3:15-16 from the Lectionary for Masses with Children #224B.

 A reading from the letter of Paul to the Colossians . . . And be grateful.

 Let the message . . . The word of the Lord.

Responsorial Psalm:

"Protect Me, O God." (Julie Howard, *Sing for Joy*, LP.)

Gospel Acclamation:

"Alleluia." (Donald J. Reagan, *Young People's Glory and Praise*, OCP.)

Gospel:

(In this gospel Jesus said to his disciples, "I give you peace.")

Presider proclaims John 14:27 from the Lectionary for Masses with Children #224.

A reading from the holy gospel according to John . . .

Homily Ideas:

We are called to live in peace with one another. We are to respect all people because they are made in the image and likeness of God. We are to follow Jesus in being peacemakers.

What are some ways we can live as people of peace?

- Listen to the ideas of other people
- Forgive those who hurt us
- Respect the rights of others
- Make up for any harm we have caused
- Treat people with kindness
- Think of several solutions to problems
- Learn about other cultures
- Speak up about wrongs to others

Pray for peace in our world. We must work to make it a reality in our lives. Peace is something for which we all must take responsibility.

General Intercessions:

The prayers are read by five children, with the assembly responding.

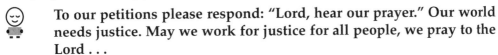 To our petitions please respond: "Lord, hear our prayer." Our world needs justice. May we work for justice for all people, we pray to the Lord . . .

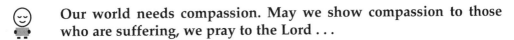 Our world needs compassion. May we show compassion to those who are suffering, we pray to the Lord . . .

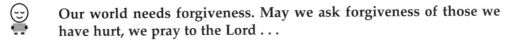 Our world needs forgiveness. May we ask forgiveness of those we have hurt, we pray to the Lord . . .

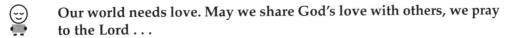 Our world needs love. May we share God's love with others, we pray to the Lord . . .

Our world needs peace. May we bring peace and hope to others, we pray to the Lord . . .

Liturgy of the Eucharist

Presentation Song:

As the table is prepared and the gifts are brought forward, we will sing "Peace Time." (Carey Landry, *Young People's Glory and Praise*, OCP.)

Presentation of the Gifts:

As the song is sung, two children carry the gifts of bread and wine to the altar and hand them to the presider.

 Wine   Bread

Eucharistic Prayer:

Eucharistic Prayer for Masses with Children II.

Eucharistic Acclamations:

"Acclamations for Prayer II." (Carey Landry, *Young People's Glory and Praise*, OCP.)

Lamb of God:

"Lamb of God." (Carey Landry, *Young People's Glory and Praise*, OCP.)

Communion Song:

As people of peace, let us join together in our communion song "Prayer of Saint Francis." (Sebastian Temple, *Young People's Glory and Praise*, OCP.)

Concluding Rite

Closing Song:

As we leave to go and live in peace, we sing together our closing song "The Peace of the Lord." (Gary Ault, Young People's Glory and Praise, OCP.)

Closing Procession:

The children who carried in the cross and children's lectionary now carry them out, accompanying the presider, as the closing song is sung.

 Cross   Children's lectionary

Peace Prayer

The children can write peace prayers during class the week before the liturgy. Stress the need to pray for peace in our world. Each prayer should read "My Peace Prayer" at the top and be signed with the individual child's name. (See p.195 for a reproducible peace prayer form.)

A Bible verse about peace such as John 14:27 can be added: "Peace I leave with you; my peace I give to you." Discuss the verse with the children.

Then ask the children to write their own individual prayer for peace and sign it. Remind the children that we are also to live as people of peace.

The peace prayers are placed in a box marked PEACE PRAYERS in large letters. The box is then carried in the entrance procession at the children's liturgy and placed by the cross. Explain that this is one way to offer the prayers for peace that are in our hearts.

NoveMbeR

REMEMBERING THE SAINTS
ALL SAINTS DAY (NOVEMBER 1)

Welcome:

This is All Saints Day. We honor all the saints who showed us how to love God and other people. We too are called to be saints in the kingdom of God. We are to follow Jesus in all that we do.

Introductory Rites

Gathering Song:

We stand and gather together as the people of God to sing "Celebrate God." (Carey Landry, *Young People's Glory and Praise*, OCP.)

Entrance Procession:

Two children accompany the presider, carrying in the cross and children's lectionary as the gathering song is sung.

 Cross   Children's lectionary

Glory to God:

"Glory to God." (Carey Landry, *Young People's Glory and Praise*, OCP.)

Liturgy of the Word

First Reading:

(In this reading John tells how he saw a crowd from every nation.)
  Child reads Revelation 7:9-10 from the Lectionary for Masses with Children #402.

 Our first reading for All Saints day is from the Book of Revelation . . .

Responsorial Psalm:

"A New Song." (Julie Howard, *Sing for Joy*, LP.)

Gospel Acclamation:

"Alleluia." (Jack Miffleton, *Young People's Glory and Praise*, OCP.)

Gospel:

(This gospel tells us about the Beatitudes.)

The presider proclaims Matthew 5:1-12 from the Lectionary for Masses with Children #402.

A reading from the holy gospel according to Matthew . . .

Homily Ideas:

Today is a day when we honor all the saints. What are the names of some of the saints? (Mary, Joseph, Francis, Patrick, Rose, Peter, Elizabeth). **Why are these people are called saints?** (They followed God's will in their lives, taught people about Jesus, helped people in need, prayed for others.)

Saints put God first in their lives and cared about other people. All of us are called to be saints. How can we become saints? (Love God and others).

Creed:

"We Believe." (*Young People's Glory and Praise*, OCP.)

Prayers of the Faithful:

Petitions are read by children.

 To our petitions, please respond: "Lord, hear our prayer." Saint Mary was chosen to be the mother of Jesus. At the cross, Jesus made her our mother, too. May we say "yes" to God as Saint Mary did, we pray to the Lord . . .

 Saint Anthony of Padua gave up a life of wealth to become a priest. He preached the word of God in a way that touched people's hearts. May we tell the good news to other people as did Saint Anthony of Padua, we pray to the Lord . . .

 Saint Clare founded a religious community. She lived a life of prayer and poverty. May we learn to be people of prayer like Saint Clare, we pray to the Lord . . .

 Saint Patrick went to Ireland to tell people about God. He used a shamrock to explain that God is Father, Son, and Holy Spirit. May we share our faith in God with others like Saint Patrick, we pray to the Lord . . .

Saint Frances Xavier Cabrini came to the United States to help people in need. She founded schools, hospitals, and orphanages. May we care about others like Saint Frances Xavier Cabrini, we pray to the Lord . . .

Liturgy of the Eucharist

Presentation Song:

As the bread and wine are brought to the altar, we will sing "God Is Building a House." (*Young People's Glory and Praise*, OCP.)

Presentation of the Gifts:

As the song is sung, two children carry the gifts of bread and wine to the altar and hand them to the presider.

 Wine   Bread

Eucharistic Prayer:

Eucharistic Prayer for Masses with Children II.

Eucharistic Acclamations:

"Acclamations for Prayer II." (Carey Landry, *Young People's Glory and Praise*, OCP.)

Communion Song:

Our song during Communion today is "Come to My Heart." (Joe Pinson, *Young People's Glory and Praise*, OCP.)

Concluding Rite

Announcement:

Thank you to the students who made the All Saints Day bulletin board for the church vestibule. It is a reminder of some of the saints we honor today. Take a look at it on the way out if you have not yet done so. (See end of liturgy for directions.)

Closing Song:

As we go to live as saints in our world, the closing song is "Great Things Happen." (Carey Landry, *Young People's Glory and Praise*, OCP.)

Closing Procession:

The children who carried in the cross and children's lectionary now carry them out, accompanying the presider, as the closing song is sung.

 Cross   Children's lectionary

Saint Bulletin Board

Students in one of the classes can create an informative All Saints Day bulletin board for the church vestibule. This project helps students learn about saints, and other classes benefit too.

For this project, items needed include a box of assorted saint holy cards, construction paper in various colors, a glue stick, scissors, a black marker, and self-stick gold crosses.

Each student should select a holy card from the assortment. Then go around the class and have each child tell something about the saint they have chosen from the information on the back of the card.

Next let each student select a half sheet of construction paper and trim it to a point at one end to look like the shape of a stained glass window. Inside each paper window the child glues the chosen holy card.

Underneath the holy card the student prints the name of the saint. Above the saint's picture they put a gold cross sticker as a sign that the saint followed Jesus.

All the saint windows are put on a bulletin board with a sign above it proclaiming "All Saints Day." This idea is a learning experience for the students who put together the bulletin board and for all who see it. The display of saints reminds us of the many people who have followed the way of Jesus in their lives.

CHANGE OUR HEARTS
31ST SUNDAY IN ORDINARY TIME (C)

Welcome:

Welcome. The gospel shows us that we are called to change our hearts because of Jesus Christ. We are to turn away from selfishness toward the light of Christ in our lives. A basket of heart cards made by some of the classes will be carried in the entrance procession. (See end of liturgy for information on heart cards.)

Introductory Rites

Gathering Song:

We join together and sing our gathering song, "Come, Follow Me." (Barbara Bridge, *Rise Up and Sing*, OCP.)

Entrance Procession:

Three children accompany the presider, carrying in the cross, children's lectionary, and heart cards as the gathering song is sung.

 Cross   Basket of heart cards   Children's lectionary

Penitential Rite:

When we sin, we turn away from God. We pray now for forgiveness for the times we did not follow the gospel. Let us pray together, saying "Lord, have mercy."

When we were unkind and impatient with others,
    Lord, have mercy.
When we did not reach out to people in need,
    Christ, have mercy.
When we did not forgive others,
    Lord, have mercy.

Liturgy of the Word

First Reading:

(In this reading we are reminded how God loves all creation.)

   Two children read Wisdom 11:22-12:1 from the Lectionary for Masses with Children #148.

 A reading from the book of Wisdom . . . we will turn to you.

 You created . . . eternal Spirit is in everything.

Responsorial Psalm:

"I Will Praise Your Name." (Robert J. Powell, *Sing Out*, WLP.)
   Children read Psalm 145:1-2, 8-9, 13-14 from the Lectionary for Masses with Children #148.

 I will praise . . . always honor your name.

 You are merciful . . . of all your creation.

 Our LORD . . . give a helping hand.

Second Reading:

(In this reading we hear that God chose us.)

   Child reads 2 Thessalonians 1:11-12 from the Lectionary for Masses with Children #148.

 A reading from the second letter of Paul to the Thessalonians . . .

Gospel Acclamation:

"Alleluia, Plant Your Word." (Christopher Walker, *Rise Up and Sing*, OCP.)

Gospel:

(Luke recounts the story of Zacchaeus.)

   The presider reads 19:1-10 from the Lectionary for Masses with Children #148.
A reading from the holy gospel according to Luke . . .

GIVE THANKS AND PRAISE

Homily Ideas:

We heard how Zacchaeus changed his life because of Jesus. We are called to be like Zacchaeus in the gospel story today. We too must change our hearts.

Zacchaeus paid back the people he had cheated. Zacchaeus said he would give money to the poor. We too must make up for any wrong we have done. We also must help those in need. We are to live as followers of Jesus Christ always.

Creed:

"We Believe." (Christopher Walker, *Rise Up and Sing*, OCP.)

General Intercessions:

The prayers are read by five children, with the assembly responding.

 To our petitions, please respond: "Lord, hear our prayer." That our hearts may be open to the needs of the poor, we pray to the Lord . . .

 That we may share what we have with other people, we pray to the Lord . . .

 That we may be fair and honest in our dealings with others, we pray to the Lord . . .

 That we will remember that all people are made in God's image and likeness, we pray to the Lord . . .

 That we may be a living gospel of God's love for all people, we pray to the Lord . . .

Liturgy of the Eucharist

Presentation Song:

Please lift up your hearts and voices in song as we sing "Each Time that You Love." (Barbara Bridge, *Rise Up and Sing*, OCP.)

Presentation of the Gifts:

As the song is sung, two children carry the gifts of bread and wine to the altar and hand them to the presider.

 Wine   Bread

Eucharistic Prayer and Acclamations:

"Eucharistic Prayer for Masses with Children II." (Christopher Walker, *Rise Up and Sing*, OCP.)

Communion Song:

As we come forward to the table of the Lord, we will sing "We Come to Share God's Special Gift." (Christopher Walker, Rise Up and Sing, OCP.)

Concluding Rite

Closing Song:

We leave today singing "We Hear God's Word." (Christopher Walker, *Rise Up and Sing*, OCP.)

Closing Procession:

The children who carried in the cross and children's lectionary now carry them out, accompanying the presider, as the closing song is sung.

 Cross   Children's lectionary

Heart Cards

The story of Zacchaeus in Luke's gospel is a story for all of us. Discuss this gospel reading in class the week before the liturgy. Explain to the children that we must allow our hearts to be touched by Jesus' forgiving love like Zacchaeus.

Ask the children in one of the grade levels to make heart cards to show that they are willing to change their hearts for Jesus. The students can cut out hearts from half-sheets of red copy-paper. Each heart should bear the statement: "Jesus, I will turn my heart and my life toward you." (See p. 196 for a reproducible heart card form.)

Ask the students to read the words on the cards out loud together. Then have each sign his or her card and place it in a wicker basket.

The basket of heart cards is carried in the entrance procession by one of the children and placed in front of the Cross.

COME BEFORE THE LORD
CHRIST THE KING (A)

Welcome:

This is the last Sunday of the church year. Today we celebrate Christ the King. We rejoice in Jesus Christ, our Lord, who is King of all. The gospel reminds us that Christ calls us to care about all people in God's kingdom. We are to see the face of Jesus in everyone we meet.

Introductory Rites

Gathering Song:

Let us now stand and sing together our gathering song, "Come, Let Us Praise Our God." (Paul Curtin, *Young People's Glory and Praise*, OCP.)

Entrance Procession:

Two children accompany the presider, carrying in the cross and children's lectionary as the gathering song is sung.

 Cross   Children's lectionary

"Glory to God." (Carey Landry, *Young People's Glory and Praise*, OCP.)

Liturgy of the Word

First Reading:

(This reading tells us that God will take good care of the people.)

   Ezekiel 34:11-12, 14-16 is read by two children from the Lectionary for Masses with Children #155.

   Our first reading is from the book of Ezekiel . . . gloomy day.

   My people . . . The word of the Lord.

Responsorial Psalm:

"The Lord Is My Shepherd." (Jane Marshall, *Sing Out*, WLP.)
Children read Psalm 23:1-2, 2-3, 5-6 from the Lectionary for Masses with Children #155.

 You, LORD . . . green grass.

 You lead me . . . right paths.

 You treat . . . in your house, Lord.

Second Reading:

(In this reading from 1 Corinthians Paul tells us that Christ will bring life to all of us.)
Three children read 15:20-24 from the Lectionary for Masses with Children #155.

 The second reading is from the first letter of Paul to the Corinthians . . . raised to life.

 Just as we . . . life to all of us.

 But we . . . The word of the Lord.

Gospel Acclamation:

"Alleluia." (Jack Miffleton, *Young People's Glory and Praise*, OCP.)

Gospel:

(This gospel proclaims that whatever we do for others, we do for Jesus.)
Presider reads Matthew 25:31-46 from the Lectionary for Masses with Children #155.
A reading from the holy gospel according to Matthew . . .

Homily Ideas:

The gospel reminds us that Jesus is King of all people and all nations. We will be judged by God on how we have helped others. We are called to see Jesus in the hungry and the sick and others in need.

Creed:

"We Believe." (Carey Landry, *Young People's Glory and Praise*, OCP.)

General Intercessions:

The prayers are read by six children, with the assembly responding. (See information on intention book at end of liturgy.)

 We offer prayers for the needs of our parish, our community and our world. To our petitions please respond: "Lord, hear our prayer." May our lives give glory to Jesus Christ who is King of all people, we pray to the Lord . . .

 May all Christians someday be united in faith, we pray to the Lord . . .

 May world leaders seek to live together in peace and harmony without war, we pray to the Lord . . .

 May the human rights of people in all nations of the world be respected, we pray to the Lord . . .

 May we work together to see that the needs of all people are met, we pray to the Lord . . .

 For all the intentions in our hearts and in our intention book, we pray to the Lord . . .

Liturgy of the Eucharist

Presentation Song:

Our song during the presentation of the gifts is "Reach Out." (Carey Landry, *Young People's Glory and Praise*, OCP.)

Presentation of the Gifts:

As the song is sung, two children carry the gifts of bread and wine to the altar and hand them to the presider.

 Wine   Bread

Eucharistic Prayer:

Eucharistic Prayer for Masses with Children II.

Eucharistic Acclamations:

"Acclamations for Prayer II." (Carey Landry, *Young People's Glory and Praise*, OCP.)

Communion Song:

As we come to the table of the Lord let us sing "You Are Near." (Dan Schutte, S.J., *Young People's Glory and Praise*, OCP.)

Concluding Rite

Closing Song:

We leave today singing praise to our God. Our closing song is "Let Heaven Rejoice." (Bob Dufford, S.J., *Young People's Glory and Praise*, OCP.)

Closing Procession:

The children who carried in the cross and children's lectionary now carry them out, accompanying the presider, as the closing song is sung.

 Cross   Children's lectionary

Intention Book

An "intention book" can be provided for the children and teachers who attend the liturgy so that they can write down their own special intentions to be remembered at Mass. These intentions can be anything from a sick relative to world peace.

A three-ring binder with a see-through insert cover is used. The title page on the front should say "Mass Intention Book" and can be decorated with a fancy border.

Inside the book, make a page for each liturgy the children will celebrate together during the year. The top of each page says "Prayer Sheet." Then lines are provided for writing. The title of the feast day or Sunday is put at the bottom of the page along with appropriate clip art or an illustration.

Explain the intention book to the children and allow them to write their special intentions on the page during class time. The book is brought to the liturgy and placed on the shelf in the prayer leader's stand or other suitable place. Then at Mass the last of the general intercessions is offered for all the intentions in the book.

This activity helps the children learn to pray for their needs and the needs of others in God's kingdom.

THANK YOU, GOD
WEEKDAY IN ORDINARY TIME

Welcome:

This week we will celebrate Thanksgiving. We remember all that God has done for us. Thanksgiving is a time to thank God for the many blessings in our lives and to share with others.

Introductory Rites

Gathering Song:

We come together as the people of God and sing "Gather Us In." (Marty Haugen, *Hymnal for Catholic Students*, GIA.)

Entrance Procession:

Two children accompany the presider, carrying in the Cross and children's lectionary as the gathering song is sung.

 Cross   Children's lectionary

Liturgy of the Word

First Reading:

(This reading reminds us to keep thanking God.)

1 Thessalonians 5:16-18 is read by child from the Lectionary for Masses with Children #219.

 A reading from the first letter of Paul to the Thessalonians . . .

Responsorial Psalm:

"A New Song." (Julie Howard, *Sing for Joy*, LP.)

Gospel Acclamation:

"Alleluia: Form B." (Marty Haugen, *Hymnal for Catholic Students*, GIA.)

Gospel:

(This gospel tells the story of Jesus curing the ten lepers.)

Presider proclaims Luke 17:11-19 from the Lectionary for Masses with Children #219.

A reading from the holy gospel according to Luke . . .

Homily Ideas:

Did you ever send thank-you notes to people? (Yes.) **To whom did you send them?** (Grandparents, neighbors.) **When?** (For birthday gifts or when someone did something nice.)

In the gospel today a leper who was cured came back to thank Jesus. We should be like that leper. We should tell God thank you for all that God has done for us. What are some of the things for which we can thank God? (Love, trees, flowers, animals, food, music, laughter, people who care about us.)

What holiday will we celebrate on Thursday? (Thanksgiving.) **What happened on the first Thanksgiving?** (The pilgrims and Indians shared food and thanked God for the harvest.) **Why do we celebrate Thanksgiving?** (To thank God for all we have been given.)

We too must share what we have been given with others. We are to share the food of the earth and all its resource. Let's remember that this Thanksgiving.

General Intercessions:

The prayers are read by five children, with the assembly responding.

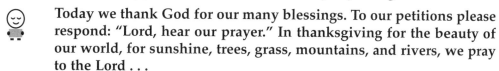

Today we thank God for our many blessings. To our petitions please respond: "Lord, hear our prayer." In thanksgiving for the beauty of our world, for sunshine, trees, grass, mountains, and rivers, we pray to the Lord . . .

In thanksgiving for all the animals of creation, for dogs and cats, zebras, lions, birds, fish, and turtles, we pray to the Lord . . .

In thanksgiving for the people who enrich our lives, for family, friends, neighbors, and classmates, we pray to the Lord . . .

In thanksgiving for the food we eat and the fresh water we drink, for medicine and health care, we pray to the Lord . . .

In thanksgiving for all the riches of the earth that we may remember that creation is a gift for all people to share, we pray to the Lord . . .

Liturgy of the Eucharist

Presentation Song:

The children will be bringing forward some of the food collected for our parish food pantry to feed the hungry. Nonperishable food is collected in boxes at the back of the church. *Four items are selected and carried forward as representative of the food donated.*

Our song during the presentation of the gifts today is "For the Beauty of the Earth." *(Hymnal for Catholic Students, GIA.)*

Presentation of the Gifts:

As the song is sung, six children carry the bread, wine, and four food items to the altar. The bread and wine are handed to the presider, and the food items are placed in a basket at the base of the processional cross.

    Food items Wine Bread

Eucharistic Prayer:

Eucharistic Prayer for Masses with Children I.

Eucharistic Acclamations:

"Mass of Creation." (Marty Haugen, *Hymnal for Catholic Students*, GIA.)

Communion Song:

As we share the eucharist together, we will sing "Gift of Finest Wheat." *(Hymnal for Catholic Students, GIA.)*

Communion Meditation:

A reflection on Thanksgiving will be presented by one of our classes. *Children come forward with letters spelling out T-H-A-N-K-S-G-I-V-I-N-G. (See end of liturgy for information.)*

Concluding Rite

Closing Song:

As we leave today, we sing God's praises. Our closing song is "Let All Things Now Living." *(Hymnal for Catholic Students, GIA.)*

Closing Procession:

The children who carried in the cross and children's lectionary now carry them out, accompanying the presider, as the closing song is sung.

 Cross   Children's lectionary

Thanksgiving Meditation

A helpful meditation can be done by a class of younger children after communion during a liturgy the week of Thanksgiving.

The prayer leader announces the meditation. Twelve children come forward. Each child holds a large card on which is printed one of the letters to spell out the word T-H-A-N-K-S-G-I-V-I-N-G. To assure visibility for both the congregation and the young reader, each card should be at least 12" x 12", with each letter being at least 9" tall.

One at a time the children read off the back of their cards something they are thankful for that begins with the letter they are holding. Following are ideas for the children:

	T	Thank you, God, for *trees.*
	H	Thank you, God, for *hands.*
	A	Thank you, God, for *animals.*
	N	Thank you, God, for *night time.*
	K	Thank you, God, for *kids.*
	S	Thank you, God, for *sunshine.*
	G	Thank you, God, for *giraffes.*
	I	Thank you, God, for *insects.*
	V	Thank you, God, for *vacation.*
	I	Thank you, God, for *ice cream.*
	N	Thank you, God, for *neighbors.*
	G	Thank you, God, for *green grass.*

When all the children are finished with their parts, they say together: "Happy Thanksgiving!"

DeCeMBeR

A SAINT FOR CHILDREN
SAINT NICHOLAS (DECEMBER 6)

Welcome:

Today we celebrate Saint Nicholas. He was a fourth-century bishop who secretly helped people. Advent is a season of giving to others. May we learn to be generous to others like Saint Nicholas.

Introductory Rites

Gathering Song:

Our gathering song is "Come Along with Me to Jesus." (Carey Landry, *Young People's Glory and Praise*, OCP.)

Entrance Procession:

Two children accompany the presider, carrying in the cross and children's lectionary as the gathering song is sung.

 Cross   Children's lectionary

Liturgy of the Word

First Reading:

(This reading tells us that God will look for the lost sheep.)

Two children read Ezekiel 34:11-16 from the Lectionary for Masses with Children #461.

 The first reading today is from the book of the prophet Ezekiel . . . wherever they settle.

 My people . . . The word of the Lord.

Responsorial Psalm:

"The Lord Is My Shepherd There Is Nothing I Shall Want." (Jane Marshall, *Sing Out*, WLP.)

Psalm 23:1-3,3-4, 6 is read by three children from the Lectionary for Masses with Children #462 no. 1.

 You, LORD. . . you refresh my life.

 You are true . . . make me feel safe.

 Your kindness . . . in your house, LORD.

Gospel Acclamation:

"Alleluia." (Jack Miffleton, *Young People's Glory and Praise*, OCP.)

Gospel:

(In this gospel Jesus calls the apostles.)

Presider reads Mark 1:14-20 from the Lectionary for Masses with Children #464, no. 2.

A reading from the holy gospel according to Mark . . .

Homily Ideas:

Today we celebrate Saint Nicholas. He gave gifts to people in secret. He helped people and he cared about children. Saint Nicholas is known as the patron saint of children.

How can we help people like Saint Nicholas did? (Stand up for someone who is being teased; help someone with their chores; say hello to a new child; play a game with a younger brother or sister; write a letter to someone who lives far away; give part of allowance or birthday money to an organization that helps children around the world; pray for children in need.)

This week, try to be like Saint Nicholas and do something for another person.

General Intercessions:

The prayers are read by five children, with the assembly responding.

 To our petitions, please respond: "Lord, hear our prayer." For children who do not have enough to eat: that others may share with them, we pray to the Lord . . .

 For children who are victims of violence: that their future may be one of hope, we pray to the Lord . . .

 For children who are sick, especially those in hospitals: that they may know that God loves them, we pray to the Lord . . .

For children who are victims of abuse or neglect: that someone will reach out a helping hand to them, we pray to the Lord . . .

 For children who live in war-torn countries: that they may find peace, we pray to the Lord . . .

Liturgy of the Eucharist

Presentation Song:

Our song during the presentation of the gifts is "Come Lord Jesus." (Carey Landry, *Young People's Glory and Praise*, OCP.)

Presentation of the Gifts:

As the song is sung, two children carry the gifts of bread and wine to the altar and hand them to the presider.

 Wine   Bread

Eucharistic Prayer:

Eucharistic Prayer for Masses with Children II.

Eucharistic Acclamations:

"Acclamations for Prayer II." (Carey Landry, *Young People's Glory and Praise*, OCP.)

Communion Song:

As we come forward to the table of the Lord let us sing "Come to My Heart." (Joe Pinson, *Young People's Glory and Praise*, OCP.)

Concluding Rite

Announcement:

Advent offering containers from the Holy Childhood Association are available at the exits today for all students. Please take one as you leave. Your contributions will help children around the world. Please bring back your offering at the end of Advent. (See end of liturgy for information on this project.)

Closing Song:

**We leave today singing together our closing song, "Children of the Lord."
(Carey Landry,** *Young People's Glory and Praise,* **OCP.)**

Closing Procession:

*The children who carried in the cross and children's lectionary now carry them out,
accompanying the presider, as the closing song is sung.*

 Cross   Children's lectionary

Giving to Others

In the spirit of Saint Nicholas, encourage students to give to others during the
Advent season. One good way to do this is by inviting participation in the
Advent appeal from Holy Childhood Association (HCA). After the Mass
honoring Saint Nicholas, have Advent offering containers from HCA available
at the exits to the church. Children can take home a collection box and
place contributions in it throughout the Advent season.

This program for kindergarten through eighth grade helps students understand their role in a universal church and to put the spirit of the season
into action.

A program guide is provided by HCA with suggestions for activities.
One idea is to show the children how much good their money can do by using comparisons. Putting the cost of two candy bars in the container will buy
twenty pairs of socks for children in developing countries. The price of three
double-scoop ice cream cones will buy four five-pound bags of rice for a hungry family.

Supplementary materials are available including posters, calendars,
videos, and newsletters. The children return the boxes to the teacher and the
donations are forwarded to HCA (1720 Massachusetts Avenue, NW, Washington, D.C. 20036).

All allocations are raised by kids to help other kids around the world.
This project helps children understand that they are part of a global community and that we are to follow the light of Christ in our hearts in reaching out
to others.

PREPARE THE WAY
SECOND SUNDAY IN ADVENT (B)

Welcome:

We gather here today to celebrate the season of Advent. We prepare our hearts and our lives for the light of Christ to come. We wait in hope for Christmas.

Introductory Rites

Gathering Song:

We stand and sing together **"Prepare Ye the Way"** (Carey Landry, *Young People's Glory and Praise, Volume Two*, OCP).

Entrance Procession:

Two children accompany the presider, carrying in the cross and children's lectionary as the gathering song is sung.

 Cross   Children's lectionary

Liturgy of the Word

First Reading:

(This reading reminds us to clear a path for the Lord.)
Two children read Isaiah 40:3-5 from the Lectionary for Masses with Children #5.

 Our reading on the Second Sunday of Advent is from the book of the prophet Isaiah . . . there for our God.

 Fill in . . . . The word of the Lord.

Responsorial Psalm:

"Lord Show Us Your Mercy."(Jack Miffleton, *Sing Out*, WLP.)
Two children read Psalm 85:8-9 and 10-11 from the Lectionary for Masses with Children #5.

I will listen . . . in all your glory.

 Love . . . from the sky above.

Gospel Acclamation:

"Alleluia." (Roc O'Connor, S.J., *Young People's Glory and Praise, Volume Two*, OCP.)

Gospel:

(In this gospel John the Baptist tells the people that Jesus is coming.)
    Presider reads Mark 1:1-8 from the Lectionary for Masses with Children #5.
The gospel we proclaim today is the beginning of the holy gospel according to Mark . . .

Homily Ideas:

What are some things we wait for? (Vacations, parties, birthdays.)

Who are we waiting for during Advent? (Jesus.)

Why did God send Jesus to us? (Because God loves us.)

How can we get ready during Advent for Jesus? (Be kind to others; pray each day; help the poor.)

We must share God's love with others.

Creed:

"We Believe in God." (Carey Landry, *Young People's Glory and Praise, Volume Two*, OCP.)

General Intercessions:

The prayers are read by five children, with the assembly responding.

 To our petitions, please respond: "Lord, hear our prayer." May we prepare our hearts and our lives as we wait for Jesus, we pray to the Lord . . .

 May we make time for other people during the busy Advent season, we pray to the Lord . . .

 May we remember those in need at this time of the year, especially the children, we pray to the Lord . . .

May we find joy in sharing, in giving, and in working together, we pray to the Lord . . .

 May we keep our focus on Jesus who is the light of the world, we pray to the Lord . . .

Liturgy of the Eucharist

Presentation Song:

As our gifts of bread and wine are brought forward, we sing "Turn to Me, My People" (Roc O'Connor, S.J. and Elizabeth Staehler, *Young People's Glory and Praise, Volume Two*, OCP).

Presentation of the Gifts:

As the song is sung, two children carry the gifts of bread and wine to the altar and hand them to the presider.

 Wine   Bread

Eucharistic Prayer:

Eucharistic Prayer for Masses with Children II.

Eucharistic Acclamations:

(Roc O'Connor, S.J. and Elizabeth Staehler, *Young People's Glory and Praise, Volume Two*, OCP.)

Communion Song:

As we come forward to share the eucharist, let us sing our communion song, "Jesus, Thank You" (Kathy Coleman and Carey Landry, *Young People's Glory and Praise, Volume Two*, OCP).

Communion Meditation:

Students will now come forward to share with us a reflection on the meaning of Advent. (See end of liturgy for script.)

Concluding Rite

Solemn Blessing:

Solemn Blessing for Advent. (From "Solemn Blessings" section of *The Sacramentary.*)

Closing Song:

We go out to prepare the way for Jesus singing "Cry Out with Gladness" (Roc O'Connor, S.J. and Elizabeth Staehler, *Young People's Glory and Praise, Volume Two*, OCP).

Closing Procession:

The children who carried in the cross and children's lectionary now carry them out, accompanying the presider, as the closing song is sung.

 Cross   Children's lectionary

Advent Reflection

After communion, six students come forward to share a reflection on the meaning of the Advent season. One at a time the children step up to the microphone and read their reflection.

 Advent is a time of waiting.

 We wait in joyful hope. We wait for Jesus to come as the Israelites waited thousands of years for a savior. We wait as Mary did for Jesus to be born in our hearts and our lives.

 Advent is a time of love.

 God loves us with an unending love. We are to share that love with others not only during this season, but throughout the year. We are to be a sign of God's love to other people.

 Advent is a time of hope.

 We trust in our God who is with us always. We are called to be a people of hope in our world.

 Advent is a time of prayer.

We thank God for the gift of Jesus and remember all that God has done for us. We pray for our needs and the needs of other people.

 Advent is a time of peace.

 We are to be peacemakers in our lives and in our world. We are to be one people with one Lord. We get ready for Jesus to come by the way we live our lives.

 Advent is a time of giving.

We share what we have and what we have been given with other people. We are to open our hearts to the needs of others. Come, Lord Jesus, come!

OUR JOURNEY OF FAITH
OUR LADY OF GUADALUPE (DECEMBER 12)

Welcome:

We come together with joy during this Advent season to celebrate the feast of Our Lady of Guadalupe. We ask Mary to walk with us on our journey of faith to the Father.

Introductory Rites

Gathering Song:

We honor Mary as we stand and join together singing our gathering song, **"Immaculate Mary."** *(Hymnal for Catholic Students, GIA.)*

Entrance Procession:

Seven children accompany the presider, carrying in the cross, children's lectionary, a picture of Our Lady of Guadalupe, a basket, and roses as the gathering song is sung. (See end of liturgy for details.)

 Cross Basket  Picture

Roses Children's Lectionary

Glory to God:

"Gloria." (Carroll T. Andrews, *Hymnal for Catholic Students*, GIA.)

Liturgy of the Word

First Reading:

(In this reading Isaiah states that those who walked in the dark have seen a bright light.)

Two children read 9:2-3,6-7 from the Lectionary for Masses with Children #447, no. 1.

 A reading from the book of the prophet Isaiah . . . are glad and celebrate.

 For us a child . . . The word of the Lord.

Responsorial Psalm:

"Bless Yahweh." (Julie Howard, *Sing for Joy*, LP.)

Second Reading:

(In this reading Paul tells the people that we are God's own adopted children.)

Ephesians 1:3-6 is read by child from the Lectionary for Masses with Children #448, no. 2.

 A reading from the letter of Paul to the Ephesians . . . innocent and loving people.

 God was kind . . . The word of the Lord.

Gospel Acclamation:

"Alleluia: Form B." (Marty Haugen, *Hymnal for Catholic Students*, GIA.)

Gospel:

(This gospel tells how Mary stood beside the cross.)

The presider reads John 19:25-27 from the Lectionary for Masses with Children #451, no 3.

A reading from the holy gospel according to John . . .

Homily Ideas:

Mary appeared to a poor Aztec Indian named Juan Diego near Mexico City. I want to share this story with you today. *Read The Lady of Guadalupe de Paola.* (See the "Resources Needed" section, p. 16.) *If there are a small number of children, invite them to sit on the altar steps as the story is read.*

Today we honor Mary as Our Lady of Guadalupe. Mary shows us that God cares about all people, especially the poor and oppressed. Today Mary still represents hope to people of all nations. We too must bring hope to all people.

General Intercessions:

The prayers are read by five children, with the assembly responding.

 To our petitions, please respond: "Lord, hear our prayer." May we celebrate all that God has done for us through Mary, we pray to the Lord . . .

 May we give Mary the honor due her as the Mother of God and our Blessed Mother, we pray to the Lord . . .

May we remember that Jesus Christ came for all people, we pray to the Lord . . .

 May we be a beacon of hope for others as Mary is for us, we pray to the Lord . . .

 May we be mindful of the needs of people of all nations, we pray to the Lord . . .

Liturgy of the Eucharist

Presentation Song:

Join in our song during the presentation of the gifts "Canticle of Mary." *(Hymnal for Catholic Students, GIA.)*

Presentation of the Gifts:

As the song is sung, two children carry the gifts of bread and wine to the altar and hand them to the presider.

 Wine   Bread

Eucharistic Prayer:

Eucharistic Prayer for Masses with Children II.

Eucharistic Acclamations:

"Mass of Creation." (Marty Haugen, *Hymnal for Catholic Students*, GIA.)

Communion Song:

As we come to the table of the Lord, we will sing "I Am the Bread of Life." (Suzanne Toolan, *Hymnal for Catholic Students*, GIA.)

Concluding Rite

Solemn Blessing:

Blessing of Blessed Virgin Mary #15. ("Solemn Blessings" section of *The Sacramentary.*)

Closing Song:

Sing out our closing song on this feast day: "Sing of Mary, Pure and Lowly." *(Hymnal for Catholic Students, GIA.)*

Closing Procession:

The children who carried in the cross and children's lectionary now carry them out, accompanying the presider, as the closing song is sung.

 Cross   Children's lectionary

Mary Procession

During the introductory rites, we gather together as the people of God. Art and other objects can be brought forward in the entrance procession to honor Mary and involve the children.

As the gathering hymn to Mary is sung by the assembly, children process in with the presider. After the cross, the next two children in the procession carry a large picture of Our Lady of Guadalupe. This is placed on a sturdy easel already in place at the side of the altar.

Next in the procession is a child with a flat wicker basket. This basket is placed in front of the picture. Then come other children. Each child carries a silk rose that is laid in the basket to honor Mary. Finally, in front of the presider the book-bearer carries the children's lectionary.

The children sit with their classmates in the assembly after the procession. The cross and book are carried out again by the same children at the end of Mass, but the other items remain to honor Mary.

TIME TO CARE
WEEKDAY IN ADVENT

Welcome:

We gather together during this Advent season to prepare for the coming of Jesus Christ. We get ready for Jesus by helping people in need and sharing God's love with others.

Introductory Rites

Gathering Song:

Stand now and join in our gathering song for Advent, "O Come, O Come, Emmanuel." *(Hymnal for Catholic Students, GIA.)*

Entrance Procession:

Two children accompany the presider, carrying in the cross and children's lectionary as the gathering song is sung.

 Cross   Children's lectionary

Liturgy of the Word

First Reading:

(This reading tells us that the Lord is our guide.)

   Child reads Isaiah 30:19-21 from the Lectionary for Masses with Children #172.

   Our reading is from the book of the prophet Isaiah . . .

Responsorial Psalm:

"To You, O Lord, I Lift My Soul." (Marty Haugen, *Hymnal for Catholic Students,* GIA.)

   Psalm 25:4-5, 8-9,10 and 14 is read by three children from the Lectionary for Masses with Children #172.

   Show me . . . You keep me safe.

You are . . . to stay on your path.

 In everything . . . with all of us.

Gospel Acclamation:

"Alleluia: Form B." (Marty Haugen, *Hymnal for Catholic Students*, GIA.)

Gospel:

(This gospel explains how Jesus told his disciples to be ready.)

    Presider reads Luke 12:35-38 from the Lectionary for Masses with Children #172.

A reading from the holy gospel according to Luke . . .

Homily Ideas:

During Advent we look forward not only to Christmas, but to the coming of Jesus Christ at the end of time. The gospel story today tells us that we must be ready. We must live as people of the kingdom of God until Jesus comes again. We must see Jesus in those around us during this Advent season and always. We must be people of peace and love.

General Intercessions:

The prayers are read by five children, with the assembly responding.

 To our petitions, please respond: "Lord, hear our prayer." For leaders of nations, that they may put aside their differences to help bring about peace in our world, we pray to the Lord . . .

 For our church, that we may walk in love and serve all people in Christ's name, we pray to the Lord . . .

 For our community, that we may reach out to those who are hurting or alone during this Advent season and always, we pray to the Lord . . .

 For the sick and suffering, that they may know the peace of God's love, we pray to the Lord . . .

 For all of us gathered here, that we may be people of caring and compassion, we pray to the Lord . . .

Liturgy of the Eucharist

Presentation Song:

Join in our song during the presentation of the gifts, "I Want to Walk as a Child of the Light." (Kathleen Thomerson, *Hymnal for Catholic Students*, GIA.)

Presentation of the Gifts:

As the song is sung, two children carry the gifts of bread and wine to the altar and hand them to the presider.

 Wine   Bread

Eucharistic Prayer:

Eucharistic Prayer for Masses with Children II.

Eucharistic Acclamations:

"Mass of Creation." (Marty Haugen, *Hymnal for Catholic Students*, GIA.)

Communion Song:

As we come to the table of the Lord, we sing together "I Am the Bread of Life." (Suzanne Toolan, *Hymnal for Catholic Students*, GIA.)

Concluding Rite

Announcement:

Thank you to those who were able to donate items for our hat-and-mitten tree in the vestibule. Remember also to pray for children in need in our community and in our world. (See end of liturgy for information on this project.)

Closing Song:

As we leave today, we sing praise to our God with our closing song, "The King of Glory." (*Hymnal for Catholic Students*, GIA.)

Closing Procession:

The children who carried in the cross and children's lectionary now carry them out, accompanying the presider, as the closing song is sung.

     Cross   Children's lectionary

Hat and Mitten Tree

During Advent, we are to reach out to others. One way to help the children do this is with a hat-and-mitten tree. In the church vestibule set up a large Christmas tree with no decorations. Encourage the children to bring warm hats and gloves and mittens to put on the tree.

Be sure to send home notes with the children at least a week before the liturgy explaining the project and the need. This will give families time to purchase an item of warm winter clothing for the tree.

Allow each classroom to come by earlier on the day of the children's liturgy to place their contributions on the tree. Thus the tree will be entirely decorated with hats and mittens when the children arrive for their Advent liturgy. Remind the children to pray for children in need also.

The hat and mitten tree is a wonderful Advent decoration for a church entryway because it reminds us of the spirit of love of this season.

After Mass, the items on the tree are donated to an organization that works with children in need in the community. This project fills a real need in a practical way.

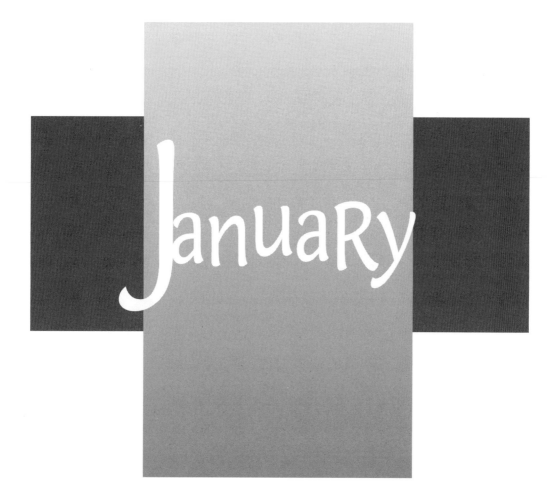

JanuaRy

SEEK THE STAR
EPIPHANY OF THE LORD

Welcome:

Welcome all of you, especially any of you who are new or visiting with us. We gather here today for the feast of Epiphany. We celebrate the journey of the wise men to see Jesus and we remember that the star of Bethlehem is a sign for all people.

Introductory Rites

Gathering Song:

On this beautiful feast day let us sing together our gathering song, "We Three Kings." (John Henry Hopkins, Jr., *Rise Up and Sing*, OCP.)

Entrance Procession:

Two children accompany the presider, carrying in the cross and children's lectionary as the gathering song is sung.

 Cross   Children's lectionary

Glory to God:

"Heritage Gloria." (Owen Alstott, *Rise Up and Sing*, OCP.)

Liturgy of the Word

First Reading:

(In this reading from Isaiah we hear how a new day is dawning for Jerusalem.)

Three children read 60:1-6 from the Lectionary for Masses with Children #16.

 A reading from the prophet Isaiah . . . light of your dawning day.

 Open your eyes . . . swell with pride.

 Treasures from over the sea. . . . The word of the Lord.

Responsorial Psalm:

"Bless Yahweh." (Julie Howard, *Sing for Joy*, LP.)

Gospel Acclamation:

"Alleluia, Shout With Joy." (Barbara Bridge and Dominic MacAller, *Rise Up and Sing*, OCP.)

Gospel:

(The gospel today tells the story of the wise men bringing gifts to Jesus.)
    The presider reads Matthew 2:1-12 from the Lectionary for Masses with Children #16.
A reading from the holy gospel according to Matthew . . .

Homily Ideas:

Did any of you get gifts for Christmas? (Yes.)

Did you give gifts? (Yes.)

Why do we give gifts to others? (To show we care about them.)

What is the feast we are celebrating today? (Epiphany.)

What happened in today's gospel story? (The wise men traveled from far away to see Jesus and bring him gifts.)

This story reminds us that Jesus came for all people and all nations.

What did the wise men follow? (A bright star.)

Whose star was it? (Jesus'.)

We too must look for Jesus in our lives. Our lives also are a journey of following Jesus.

Creed:

"We Believe." (Christopher Walker, *Rise Up and Sing*, OCP.)

General Intercessions:

The prayers are read by five children, with the assembly responding.

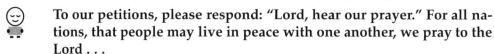 **To our petitions, please respond: "Lord, hear our prayer." For all nations, that people may live in peace with one another, we pray to the Lord . . .**

For the church throughout the world, that we may be a sign of God's love to all, we pray to the Lord . . .

For all travelers, that they may reach their destinations safely, we pray to the Lord . . .

For all children, that they may we welcomed with love as was the Christ child, we pray to the Lord . . .

For all of us gathered here, that we may follow the star of Jesus in our lives, we pray to the Lord . . .

Liturgy of the Eucharist

Presentation Song:

Our song during the presentation of the gifts is "What Child Is This." (William Chatterton, *Rise Up and Sing*, OCP.)

Presentation of the Gifts:

As the song is sung, two children carry the gifts of bread and wine to the altar and hand them to the presider.

 Wine   Bread

Eucharistic Prayer and Acclamations:

"Eucharistic Prayer for Masses with Children II." (Christopher Walker, *Rise Up and Sing*, OCP.)

Communion Song:

As we come forward for communion or for a blessing, we will sing together, "We Come to Share God's Special Gift." (Christopher Walker, *Rise Up and Sing*, OCP.)

Communion Meditation:

One of the classes will now lead us in singing "Silent Night." Please join in the singing and the gestures. (See end of liturgy for song motions.) *If there are children older than third grade present, you may want to indicate that you hope they will be able to help the younger children in learning these motions.*

Concluding Rite

Solemn Blessing:

Solemn Blessing for Epiphany. (From *The Sacramentary*.)

Closing Song:

Sing out our closing song today, "Hark! The Herald Angels Sing." (Charles Wesley and Felix Mendelssohn, *Rise Up and Sing,* OCP.)

Closing Procession:

The children who carried in the cross and children's lectionary now carry them out, accompanying the presider, as the closing song is sung.

 Cross   Children's lectionary

Carol with Gestures

As a communion meditation, one of the younger classes can lead the other children in singing the song "Silent Night," with the following gestures. The motions help the children understand the meaning of this traditional Christmas carol. The following gestures can be used:

Silent night, holy night,	(hands folded in prayer)
All is calm, all is bright.	(arms out in front)
Round yon Virgin, Mother and Child.	(hands over heart)
Holy Infant, so tender and mild,	(cradle arms)
Sleep in heavenly peace,	(hands next to head)
Sleep in heavenly peace.	
Silent night, holy night,	(hands folded in prayer)
Shepherds quake at the sight	(arms crossed by face)
Glories stream from heaven afar,	(move arms in circle)
Heavenly hosts sing alleluia.	(hands next to mouth)
Christ the Savior is born,	(arms overhead)
Christ the Savior is born.	

A TEACHER OF CHILDREN
SAINT ELIZABETH ANN SETON (JANUARY 4)

Welcome:

On this day we honor Elizabeth Ann Seton. She was a person of great faith who treated others with forgiveness and love. She is an American saint who was a teacher of children and also founded a school.

Introductory Rites

Gathering Song:

Join together in singing our gathering song, "Gather Us In." (Marty Haugen, *Hymnal for Catholic Students*, GIA.)

Entrance Procession:

Two children accompany the presider, carrying in the cross and children's lectionary as the gathering song is sung.

 Cross   Children's lectionary

Liturgy of the Word

First Reading:

(In this reading from Philippians, Paul tells people to keep their minds on what is true.)

Two children read 4:4-9 from the Lectionary for Masses with Children #470, no. 4.

 A reading from the letter of Paul to the Philippians . . . the way you think and feel.

 Finally . . . The word of the Lord.

Responsorial Psalm:

"Taste and see the goodness of the Lord." (Richard Proulx, *Hymnal for Catholic Students*, GIA.)

Three children read Psalm 34:1-2,3-4,8-9 from the Lectionary for Masses with Children #471, no. 1.

 I will always . . . listen and be glad.

 Honor the LORD . . . from all my fears.

 Discover . . . will ever be in need.

Gospel Acclamation:

"Alleluia: Form B." (Marty Haugen, *Hymnal for Catholic Students*, GIA.)

Gospel:

(This gospel tells us that we must be humble as a child to get into the king-dom of heaven.)

Presider reads Matthew 18:1-4 from the Lectionary for Masses with Children #473, no. 1.

A reading from the holy gospel according to Matthew . . .

Homily Ideas:

Today we honor Saint Elizabeth Ann Seton. This American saint was born in New York City. I would like to share with you a little of the story of her life. *Read about Saint Elizabeth Ann Seton from* Saints for All Seasons *by Sr. Mary Fearon.* (See the "Resources Needed" section, p. 16.)

Elizabeth always tried to do the will of God. We should try to do what God wants in our lives too.

General Intercessions:

The prayers are read by five children, with the assembly responding.

 To our petitions please respond: "Lord, hear our prayer." For teachers, that they may be patient with the children in their care, we pray to the Lord . . .

 For students of all ages, that they may seek God in everything they do, we pray to the Lord . . .

 For parents, that they may show children how to love God by their example, we pray to the Lord . . .

For the sick, that they may feel the healing touch of the Lord's presence in their lives, we pray to the Lord . . .

 For those who have suffered the death of a family member, that they may be comforted, we pray to the Lord . . .

Liturgy of the Eucharist

Presentation Song:

Today, along with the bread and wine, the children will bring forward a basket with some of the school supplies collected for our sister school. (See end of liturgy for information.)

Join in singing our presentation song as the gifts are brought forward, **"Now Thank We All Our God."** (*Hymnal for Catholic Students*, GIA.)

Presentation of the Gifts:

As the song is sung, three children carry the bread, wine, and basket of school supplies to the altar. The bread and wine are handed to the presider, and the basket of school supplies is placed at the base of the processional cross.

 Basket of school supplies   Wine   Bread

Eucharistic Prayer:

Eucharistic Prayer for Masses with Children II.

Eucharistic Acclamations:

"Mass of Creation." (Marty Haugen, *Hymnal for Catholic Students*, GIA.)

Communion Song:

Let us sing together our song during Communion today, **"Jesu, Jesu, Fill Us with Your Love."** (*Hymnal for Catholic Students*, GIA.)

Concluding Rite

Closing Song:

As we go forth to share the good news, we will sing **"Let Us Walk in the Light."** (Marty Haugen, *Hymnal for Catholic Students*, GIA.)

Closing Procession:

The children who carried in the cross and children's lectionary now carry them out, accompanying the presider, as the closing song is sung.

 Cross   Children's lectionary

School Supplies Offering

Saint Elizabeth Ann Seton was a teacher who cared about children. In her name we can also reach out to other children by collecting school supplies. At least a week before the liturgy, send home a note with the children asking for donations of new school supplies for another school with limited resources.

Schools often find that the families of some children do not have the necessary supplies to do their school work and cannot afford to purchase all that are needed. Especially halfway through the year, children may have used up all the supplies they had in the beginning of the school year.

Pens, pencils, notebook paper, rulers, and other school supplies can be collected for another school as a service project. Provide boxes in the back of the church for the donations. Also put sample items in a basket and let one of the children carry it in procession during the presentation of the gifts.

This can be part of an ongoing project throughout the year for a school with much to offer to share with another school that doesn't have as much. Contact the diocesan office for information on such a "twinning" project.

GIVING OF OURSELVES
WEEKDAY IN ORDINARY TIME

Welcome:

Welcome! The gospel calls us to use the gifts God has given us for the good of others. We are to be good stewards of all our gifts. In our entrance procession, "stewardship cards" will be brought forward which were made by some of the children as signs of what they will do for others in Jesus' name. (See end of liturgy for description of cards.)

Introductory Rites

Gathering Song:

Join in our gathering song as we stand and sing together "Part of a Circle." (Ray Repp, *Young People's Glory and Praise, Volume Two*, OCP.)

Entrance Procession:

Three children accompany the presider, carrying in the cross, children's lectionary, and basket of stewardship cards as the gathering song is sung.

 Cross   Children's lectionary   Basket of stewardship cards

Liturgy of the Word

First Reading:

(In the reading from the first letter of Peter we are reminded to give our gifts in service of others.)

Child reads 4:10-11 from the Lectionary for Masses with Children #202.

 A reading from the first letter of Peter . . .

Responsorial Psalm:

"Protect Me, O God." (Julie Howard, *Sing for Joy*, LP.)

Gospel Acclamation:

"Speak, Lord." (Jack Miffleton, *Young People's Glory and Praise, Volume Two,* OCP.)

Gospel:

(This is the story of the faithful servant.)
   Presider reads Matthew 25:14-29 from the Lectionary for Masses with Children #202.
A reading from the holy gospel according to Matthew . . .

Homily Ideas:

Everything we are is a gift from God who created us. God gave us talents to use for the good of all people. In the gospel story today the servant who used his gifts is praised by the master. We too are to give willingly to others.

   We are to give of our time, our talent, and our treasure. We can give our time by helping others, we can share our talents with our community, and we can give money to aid people in need.

   We need to ask ourselves two questions today: (1) What are my gifts? (2) How can I use these talents for the good of others?

General Intercessions:

The prayers are read by five children, with the assembly responding.

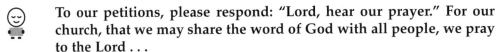 To our petitions, please respond: "Lord, hear our prayer." For our church, that we may share the word of God with all people, we pray to the Lord . . .

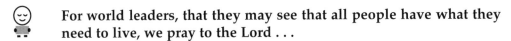 For world leaders, that they may see that all people have what they need to live, we pray to the Lord . . .

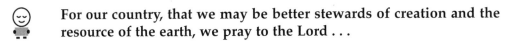 For our country, that we may be better stewards of creation and the resource of the earth, we pray to the Lord . . .

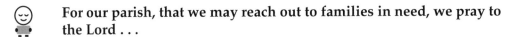 For our parish, that we may reach out to families in need, we pray to the Lord . . .

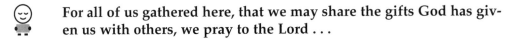 For all of us gathered here, that we may share the gifts God has given us with others, we pray to the Lord . . .

Liturgy of the Eucharist

Presentation Song:

As the gifts of bread and wine are brought to the table, we will sing together "We Are Your Hands." (Larry Folk, *Young People's Glory and Praise, Volume Two*, OCP.)

Presentation of the Gifts:

As the song is sung, two children carry the gifts of bread and wine to the altar and hand them to the presider.

 Wine   Bread

Eucharistic Prayer:

Eucharistic Prayer for Masses with Children II.

Eucharistic Acclamations:

(Roc O'Connor, S.J. and Elizabeth Staehler, *Young People's Glory and Praise, Volume Two*, OCP.)

Communion Song:

As we share the eucharist together, let us sing "A Gift from Your Children." (Nancy Bourassa and Carey Landry, *Young People's Glory and Praise, Volume Two*, OCP.)

Concluding Rite

Closing Song:

We leave today to go and live as the people of God. Our closing song is "The Greatest Gift." (Carey Landry, *Young People's Glory and Praise, Volume Two*, OCP.)

Closing Procession:

The children who carried in the cross and children's lectionary now carry them out, accompanying the presider, as the closing song is sung.

 Cross   Children's lectionary

Stewardship Cards

Stewardship is the responsibility of all of us. All that we have and all that we are is a gift from God. As the servant in Matthew's gospel used his gifts wisely, so we too are to be good stewards of God's creation. God intends that we are to use our gifts to build up the kingdom of God. One way to encourage students to think about giving of themselves is with "stewardship cards."

The concept of stewardship should be discussed in class the week before the liturgy. Students talk about what they can do for others with their time, talent, or treasure.

Then each student is asked to fill out a stewardship card indicating their own personal pledge. The card states: "I will give to other people by . . ." The student lists her or his own ideas for service and then signs the card. (See p. 197 for a reproducible stewardship card form.)

The students place their completed stewardship cards in a basket. At the children's liturgy the basket of cards is brought forward in the entrance procession and placed in front of the cross.

THE MISSION OF JESUS
THIRD SUNDAY IN ORDINARY TIME (C)

Welcome:

We gather together during this season of ordinary time to remember all that God has done for us. Jesus Christ was sent by the Father. Through the Holy Spirit, the mission of Jesus to all people will be accomplished.

Introductory Rites

Gathering Song:

Sing out our gathering song, "Awake! Arise, and Rejoice." (Marie-Jo Thum, *Rise Up and Sing*, OCP.)

Entrance Procession:

Two children accompany the presider, carrying in the cross and children's lectionary as the gathering song is sung.

 Cross   Children's lectionary

Glory to God:

"Heritage Gloria." (Owen Alstott, *Rise Up and Sing*, OCP.) *Use gestures to enhance the meaning of this prayer for children.* (See end of liturgy for information.) *If there are children older than third grade present, you may want to ask the older children to help the younger children learn the motions.*

Liturgy of the Word

First Reading:

(In this reading from Nehemiah, we hear how the people listened to the law of Moses read to them.)

Three children read 8:1-4, 5-6, 8-10 from the Lectionary for Masses with Children #64.

 A reading from the book of Nehemiah . . . built for him.

The platform . . . what it meant.

 Then Nehemiah . . . The word of the Lord.

Responsorial Psalm:

"A New Song." (Julie Howard, *Sing for Joy*, LP.)

Second Reading:

(In this reading from 1 Corinthians, Paul tells us that we are each part of the body of Christ.)

Child reads 12:12-14,27 from the Lectionary for Masses with Children #64.

 A reading from the First Letter of Paul to the Corinthians . . .

Gospel Acclamation:

"Alleluia! Plant Your Word." (Christopher Walker, *Rise Up and Sing*, OCP.)

Gospel:

(This gospel tells the story of Jesus reading from scripture in the Temple.)

Presider reads Luke 4:14-21 from the Lectionary for Masses with Children #64.

A reading from the holy gospel according to Luke . . .

Homily Ideas:

In the gospel reading today, we heard how Jesus taught the people in the temple. The words of the Old Testament are fulfilled in Jesus. Jesus showed he was God by everything he did. Jesus taught the people and performed public miracles.

Jesus' mission is to all people. The gospel tells us that Jesus had the power of the Spirit. We too have the Holy Spirit to guide our lives. We are called to follow Jesus and to tell everyone the good news.

Creed:

"We Believe in God." (Frank Alleruzzo, *Rise Up and Sing*, OCP.)

General Intercessions:

The prayers are read by five children, with the assembly responding.

 To our petitions, please respond: "Lord, hear our prayer." May we re-member how much God loves us to send us his Son, Jesus, we pray to the Lord . . .

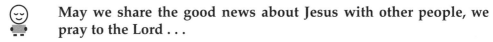

May we share the good news about Jesus with other people, we pray to the Lord . . .

May we show care and concern for others as Jesus did, we pray to the Lord . . .

May we be open to the Holy Spirit at work in our lives, we pray to the Lord . . .

May we carry on the mission of Jesus to all people, we pray to the Lord . . .

Liturgy of the Eucharist

Presentation Song:

As the gifts are brought forward and the table is prepared, we will sing **"Because of Jesus."** (Barbara Bridge, *Rise Up and Sing,* OCP.)

Presentation of the Gifts:

As the song is sung, two children carry the gifts of bread and wine to the altar and hand them to the presider.

 Wine   Bread

Eucharistic Prayer and Acclamations:

"Eucharistic Prayer for Masses with Children II." (Christopher Walker, *Rise Up and Sing,* OCP.)

Communion Song:

As we come forward together to the table of the Lord, we will sing together our communion song "One Lord." (Scott Soper, *Rise Up and Sing,* OCP.)

Concluding Rite

Closing Song:

We leave today singing praise to our God. Our closing song is "You Are My Hope." (Marie-Jo Thum, *Rise Up and Sing,* OCP.)

Closing Procession:

The children who carried in the cross and children's lectionary now carry them out, accompanying the presider, as the closing song is sung.

 Cross   Children's lectionary

Glory to God

The Gloria is an ancient prayer that helps us praise our God together. Gestures encourage children to think about the meaning of the words they are praying. Use the gestures below as the Gloria is sung or recited by the assembly. An adult should stand at the front to lead the gestures.

Glory to God in the highest,	(arms open wide)
and peace to his people on earth.	(hands clasped together)
Lord God, heavenly King,	(arms open wide)
almighty God and Father,	(arms overhead)
we worship you, we give you thanks,	(hands folded in prayer)
we praise you for your glory.	(arms open wide)
Lord Jesus Christ, only Son of the Father,	(point to either palm)
Lord God, Lamb of God,	(arms open wide)
you take away the sin of the world:	(arms forward, palms up)
have mercy on us;	(fold hands together)
you are seated at the right hand	
of the Father:	(arms overhead)
receive our prayer.	(head bowed, hands folded in prayer)
For you alone are the Holy One,	(arms outstretched)
you alone are the Lord,	(arms forward, palms up)
You alone are the Most High,	(head bowed, hands folded)
Jesus Christ,	(point to palms)
with the Holy Spirit,	(hands over heart)
in the glory of God the Father.	(arms overhead)
Amen.	(head bowed, arms at side)

FeBRuAry

FAITH IN GOD
WEEKDAY IN ORDINARY TIME

Welcome:

Welcome to our liturgy. Today we remember that we are to have faith in Jesus Christ. We are called to be people of faith in all things. Faith helps us to see things as they really are. Faith enables us to see with our hearts. With faith we can become all that God created us to be.

Introductory Rites

Gathering Song:

We come together as the people of God and join in singing our gathering song, "Come, Follow Me." (Barbara Bridge, *Rise Up and Sing*, OCP.)

Entrance Procession:

Three children accompany the presider, carrying in the cross, children's lectionary, and faith poster as the gathering song is sung. (See end of liturgy for instructions on poster.)

 Cross   Poster   Children's lectionary

Liturgy of the Word

First Reading:

(In this reading, we are told that the Lord will lead the blind.)
    Child reads Isaiah 42:16 from the Lectionary for Masses with Children #208.

 A reading from the book of the prophet Isaiah . . .

Responsorial Psalm:

"The Lord Is My Light and My Salvation." (Dolores Hruby, *Sing Out*, WLP.)
    Psalm 27:1, 8,and 11 is read from the Lectionary for Masses with Children #208.

 You, LORD . . . I have no fears.

My heart . . . on the right path.

Gospel Acclamation:

"Alleluia, Plant Your Word." (Christopher Walker, *Rise Up and Sing*, OCP.)

Gospel:

(This gospel is the story of Jesus curing blind Bartimaeus.)
The presider reads Mark 10:46-52 from the Lectionary for Masses with Children #208.
A reading from the holy gospel according to Mark . . .

Homily Ideas:

What does this poster say? (Faith)
Today I want to read to you a little book called *What Is Faith?* (See the "Resources Needed" section, p. 16.)
The gospel story today is about faith. In this story Bartimaeus was a blind man. But he could see with his heart. He believed in Jesus Christ. There were many people around Bartimaeus who could see, but they did not have faith. They were blind to who Jesus was.
We need to be like Bartimaeus and have faith in Jesus. We must learn to see with our hearts. We must learn what is really important in life.
Jesus cured the man's blindness. Then he followed Jesus. We are to be like Bartimaeus and follow the way of Jesus in our lives.

General Intercessions:

The prayers are read by five children, with the assembly responding.

 As people of faith, we offer our prayers together. To our petitions, please respond: "Lord, hear our prayer." May we always have faith in God even in difficult times, we pray to the Lord . . .

 May we reach out with understanding to all those who have disabilities, we pray to the Lord . . .

 May we see with our hearts as well as our eyes, we pray to the Lord . . .

 May we follow the light of Christ in our lives wherever it leads us, we pray to the Lord . . .

 May all people may find hope in Jesus Christ, we pray to the Lord . . .

Liturgy of the Eucharist

Presentation Song:

Lift up your voices in song during the presentation of the gifts, singing "Because of Jesus." (Barbara Bridge, *Rise Up and Sing*, OCP.)

Presentation of the Gifts:

As the song is sung, two children carry the gifts of bread and wine to the altar and hand them to the presider.

 Wine    Bread

Eucharistic Prayer and Acclamations:

"Eucharistic Prayer for Masses with Children II." (Christopher Walker, *Rise Up and Sing*, OCP.)

Communion Song:

As people of faith, let us sing together our song during communion, "I, the Lord." (Owen Alstott, *Rise Up and Sing*, OCP.)

Concluding Rite

Closing Song:

We go forth as the people of God as we sing together our closing song, "Light of the World." (Jennie Flack, *Rise Up and Sing*, OCP.)

Closing Procession:

The children who carried in the cross and children's lectionary now carry them out, accompanying the presider, as the closing song is sung.

 Cross   Children's lectionary

Faith Poster

A poster can be made to help the children remember that the story of the blind man is one about faith in Jesus Christ. Visual aids help in understanding and remembering Bible stories.

Ask a small class of older students to make this poster using red letters to spell the word FAITH in capital letters on white poster board.

Enlarge the letter patterns found on p. 198 on a copy machine. The pattern for each letter is placed on top of red construction paper. Then the students use the pattern as a guide to neatly cut out the letters.

Next the students attach the letters to the poster board using a glue stick. The letters should be large enough and bright enough to be viewed by the children in the assembly from a distance.

The poster is carried in the entrance procession. It is placed on an easel so it will be visible throughout the liturgy. The presider can also call attention to the poster during the homily.

LOVE OUR ENEMIES
7TH SUNDAY IN ORDINARY TIME (C)

Welcome:

The message of Jesus is one of love. We are reminded that Jesus calls us to love all people, even our enemies. We must reach out to others as Jesus showed us.

Introductory Rites

Gathering Song:

We stand to sing together our gathering song, "Spirit of God, Come to Us." (Sr. Veronica McGrath and Carey Landry, *Young People's Glory and Praise, Volume Two*, OCP.)

Entrance Procession:

Two children accompany the presider, carrying in the cross and children's lectionary as the gathering song is sung.

 Cross   Children's lectionary

Penitential Rite:

We now tell Jesus we are sorry for the times we have not followed the way of love. "Penitential Rite II." (Donald J. Reagan, *Young People's Glory and Praise, Volume Two*, OCP.)

Liturgy of the Word

First Reading:

(This reading is the story of David and Saul.)

Two children read Samuel 26:2, 7-9, 12-13, 22-23 from the Lectionary for Masses with Children #76.

 A reading from the first book of Samuel . . . who kills his chosen king.

David took. . . . The word of the Lord.

Responsorial Psalm:

"The Lord Is Kind and Merciful." ("Psalms for All Seasons: Set 2", Carey Landry, *Young People's Glory and Praise, Volume Two*, OCP.)

 Two children read Psalm 103:1-2, 3 and 13 from the Lectionary for Masses with Children #76.

 With all my heart . . . how kind he has been.

 The LORD forgives . . . to all who worship him.

Gospel Acclamation:

"Speak, Lord." (Jack Miffleton, *Young People's Glory and Praise, Volume Two*, OCP.)

Gospel:

(In this gospel Jesus tells us to love even our enemies.)

 Presider reads Luke 6:27-37 from the Lectionary for Masses with Children #76.

A reading from the holy gospel according to Luke . . .

Homily Ideas:

In today's gospel, Jesus tells us that we are to love even our enemies and be good to them. This is difficult to do, but following Jesus is not easy. This gospel challenges us to become all that we are capable of being as God's creation. We are to try to be peacemakers in our lives and in the world.

Peace Ceremony:

Commitment to Peace. (See end of liturgy for ceremony.)

General Intercessions:

The prayers are read by five children, with the assembly responding.

 We pray today for the needs of our church and our world. To our petitions, please respond: "Lord, hear our prayer." For all Christians: that we may see Jesus in the face of every person we meet, we pray to the Lord . . .

For all those who suffer from prejudice and discrimination: that they may not harden their hearts, we pray to the Lord . . .

 For all of us gathered here today: that we may love even our enemies as Jesus taught, we pray to the Lord . . .

 For leaders of all nations: that they may learn to live in peace, we pray to the Lord . . .

For our church: that we may work for justice for all people, we pray to the Lord . . .

Liturgy of the Eucharist

Presentation Song:

Join in our song during the presentation of the gifts, "A Gift from Your Children." (Nancy Bourassa and Carey Landry, *Young People's Glory and Praise, Volume Two*, OCP.)

Presentation of the Gifts:

As the song is sung, two children carry the gifts of bread and wine to the altar and hand them to the presider.

 Wine   Bread

Eucharistic Prayer:

Eucharistic Prayer for Masses with Children II.

Eucharistic Acclamations:

(Roc O'Connor, S.J. and Elizabeth Staehler, *Young People's Glory and Praise, Volume Two*, OCP.)

Communion Song:

Let us lift our voices in song as we sing our communion song, "Receive Our Prayer." (Carey Landry, *Young People's Glory and Praise*, OCP.)

Concluding Rite

Closing Song:

We leave today to go and live as people of peace and love, singing "We Are Your Hands." (Larry Folk, *Young People's Glory and Praise, Volume Two,* OCP.)

Closing Procession:

The children who carried in the cross and children's lectionary now carry them out, accompanying the presider, as the closing song is sung.

 Cross   Children's lectionary

Commitment to Peace

After the homily, the presider asks everyone to stand and participate in a ceremony of commitment to peace. This activity reminds the students of their responsibilities to live in peace with all people as Jesus taught us. The peace ceremony is placed in a three-ring binder so that the presider can easily read it after the homily. The presider reads the introduction and then the statements one at a time. The children respond "We will" to each statement.

We gather here today in the name of Jesus Christ, our Lord. Jesus calls each of us to live in peace and to love one another. At this time, we ask you to stand and commit yourselves to living as people of peace. We will respond together by saying "We will."

Will you treat other people with respect?

(Response: We will.)

Will you be fair even to those you do not like?

(Response: We will.)

Will you listen to what others have to say?

(Response: We will.)

Will you try to forgive those who hurt you?

(Response: We will.).

Will you help the poor and suffering in Jesus' name?

(Response: We will.)

Will you work for peace in our world?

(Response: we will.)

You have pledged to live in peace with one another. When you leave today remember to live always as Jesus taught us.

OUR JOURNEY THROUGH LENT
ASH WEDNESDAY

Welcome:

This is Ash Wednesday. We begin our forty-day journey through Lent toward the light of Easter. Lent is to be a time of growth and renewal for all of us. Ashes will be distributed after the homily. We will be signed with the cross as a reminder to follow Jesus.

Introductory Rites

Gathering Song:

Let us stand and sing together our gathering song for Lent, "Again We Keep this Solemn Fast" (*Hymnal for Catholic Students*, GIA).

Entrance Procession:

Two children accompany the presider, carrying in the cross and children's lectionary as the gathering song is sung.

 Cross   Children's lectionary

Liturgy of the Word

First Reading:

(Today's first reading reminds us that we are to share with those in need.)

Three children read Isaiah 58:6-9 from the Lectionary for Masses with Children #176.

 The first reading today is from the prophet Isaiah . . . who are abused!

 Share your food . . . your relatives.

 Then your light . . . The word of the Lord.

Responsorial Psalm:

"The Lord Is My Light and My Salvation." (David Haas, *Hymnal for Catholic Students*, GIA.)

Psalm 27:1, 11, 13 is read by children from the Lectionary for Masses with Children #176.

 You, LORD . . . I have no fears.

 Teach me . . . how kind you are.

Gospel Acclamation:

"Praise to You." (Frank Schoen, *Hymnal for Catholic Students*, GIA.)

Gospel:

(In this gospel Jesus tells us to do good deeds in secret so only the Father can see us.)

Presider proclaims Matthew 6:1-4 from the Lectionary for Masses with Children #176.

Let us listen now to a reading from the holy gospel according to Matthew . . .

Homily Ideas:

What season are we beginning today? (Lent.) **How long does Lent last?** (forty days.) **In a few minutes everyone will be invited to come forward so that ashes can be placed on your foreheads. Why are ashes put in the shape of a cross?** (To remind us of Jesus.)

As ashes are given, the words said are "Turn away from sin and be faithful to the Gospel." What are ways we can be faithful to the teachings of Jesus during Lent? (Be kind to others; forgive those who have hurt us; help other people; try to be people of peace; donate to Operation Rice Bowl; read Bible stories about Jesus; pray for others.)

Blessing and Giving of Ashes:

(The prayers for the blessing and distribution of ashes for Ash Wednesday are found in *The Sacramentary*.) *Bowls of ashes should be placed on a separate table before Mass begins.*

You may now come forward to be given ashes. ("Jesu, Jesu, Fill Us with Your Love," *Hymnal for Catholic Students*, GIA, instrumental only.)

General Intercessions:

The prayers are read by five children, with the assembly responding.

We bring our intentions before God. To our petitions please respond: "Lord, hear our prayer." During these forty days may we pick up our cross and follow Jesus, we pray to the Lord . . .

 May we forgive others who hurt us as God forgives us, we pray to the Lord . . .

 May we give from our hearts what we have so that other people will have what they need, we pray to the Lord . . .

 May we remember to pray not only for our needs, but for the needs of others, we pray to the Lord . . .

 During this season of Lent may we grow in faith, hope and love of God, we pray to the Lord . . .

Liturgy of the Eucharist

Presentation Song:

Our song today during the presentation of the gifts is "Bring Forth the Kingdom." (Marty Haugen, *Hymnal for Catholic Students*, GIA.)

Presentation of the Gifts:

As the song is sung, two children carry the gifts of bread and wine to the altar and hand them to the presider.

 Wine  Bread

Eucharistic Prayer:

Eucharistic Prayer for Masses with Children II.

Eucharistic Acclamations:

"Mass of Creation." (Marty Haugen, *Hymnal for Catholic Students*, GIA.)

Communion Song:

As we come forward to receive Jesus in the eucharist, we will sing "Let Us Break Bread Together." (*Hymnal for Catholic Students*, GIA.)

Concluding Rite

Announcement:

After Mass today you may choose a cross off our Lenten tree. Please carry out the action printed on the cross. Return the yarn from the cross at the next liturgy and tie it in a bow on the tree. (See end of liturgy for information.)

Closing Song:

As we leave today to begin our Lenten journey, let us sing "Lord Who Throughout These Forty Days." (*Hymnal for Catholic Students*, GIA.)

Closing Procession:

The children who carried in the cross and children's lectionary now carry them out, accompanying the presider, as the closing song is sung.

 Cross   Children's lectionary

Lenten Trees

The Lenten tree idea helps students live the spirit of the season. This project encourages the children to pray and do good works during Lent.

This idea is described in the article, "Fruitful Lenten Trees" in *Catechist* by Sr. Frances Chirco. A potted live tree or a silk tree is set up in the church vestibule or at the entrance to the liturgy space. Purple paper crosses are hung from the tree with yarn.

On each cross is printed a Lenten practice to do during the coming week of Lent. Examples are:

Thank God for one thing each day
Help someone without being asked
Say the Our Father
Read Psalm 117
Contribute to Operation Rice Bowl
Pray for the homeless

Each week the children return the purple yarn from their crosses and tie it in a bow on the tree. They choose another cross for the following week. Soon the tree will be covered with yarn bows as a sign of our Lenten journey as followers of Jesus.

PRAYING TO GOD
WEEKDAY IN LENT

Welcome:

We come together during this season of Lent to remember that we are to be people of prayer. Prayer is our response to God's love. Through prayer we praise God and ask for what we need. We should pray, always giving glory to God in all that we say and do.

Introductory Rites

Gathering Song:

Our gathering song today is "All That We Have." (Gary Ault, *Young People's Glory and Praise*, OCP.)

Entrance Procession:

Two children accompany the presider, carrying in the cross and children's lectionary as the gathering song is sung.

 Cross   Children's lectionary

Liturgy of the Word

First Reading:

(In this reading, Paul urges us to love and forgive others.)
Child reads Colossians 3:12-14 from the Lectionary for Masses with Children #178.

 A reading from the letter of Paul to the Colossians . . .

Responsorial Psalm:

"Be Merciful, O Lord, for We Have Sinned." (James V. Marcheonda, O.P., *Sing Out*, WLP.)
Psalm 51:1,10,12,15 is read by two children from the Lectionary for Masses with Children #178.

You are . . . faithful again.

 Make me . . . praise you, Lord.

Gospel Acclamation:

"Lenten Gospel Acclamation." (Joe Regan, *Young People's Glory and Praise*.)

Gospel:

(In this gospel Jesus teaches us the Our Father.)
   Presider reads Matthew 6:7-15 from the Lectionary for Masses with Children #178.
A reading from the holy gospel according to Matthew . . .

Homily Ideas:

During Lent and at all times we are to be people of prayer. Jesus taught us to pray the Our Father. In this prayer we pray to God who is the Father of all of us and loves us. We honor God with this prayer. We say in the Our Father that we will try to do what God wants us to do. We ask God to forgive us as we forgive others.

   What are some other ways to pray? (By singing, by saying the rosary, in our own words.) **Where are some places we can pray?** (At home, at school, outside, in church.) **When are some times when we pray?** (At mealtimes, at bedtime, in the morning.) **Remember that we can pray to God when we are happy, or sad, or afraid, or anytime.**

General Intercessions:

The prayers are read by five children, with the assembly responding.

 To our petitions, please respond: "Lord, hear our prayer." For the needs of all people the world over, we pray to the Lord . . .

 For joy in doing the will of God, we pray to the Lord . . .

 For the intentions of ourselves and our families, we pray to the Lord . . .

 For forgiveness for our failings and our selfishness, we pray to the Lord . . .

 For lives that give glory to God in all we do, we pray to the Lord . . .

Liturgy of the Eucharist

Presentation Song:

As the table is prepared and the gifts are brought forward, let us sing **"Come to My Heart."** (Joe Pinson, *Young People's Glory and Praise*, OCP.)

Presentation of the Gifts:

As the song is sung, two children carry the gifts of bread and wine to the altar and hand them to the presider.

 Wine   Bread

Eucharistic Prayer:

Eucharistic Prayer for Masses with Children II.

Eucharistic Acclamations:

"Acclamations for Prayer II." (*Carey Landry, Young People's Glory and Praise,* OCP.)

Our Father:

"The Our Father." (Carey Landry, *Young People's Glory and Praise*, OCP.) *This prayer can be enhanced when sung or said if the children are led in gestures. (See end of liturgy for directions.) If there are children older than third grade present, you may want to ask the older children to help the younger children to learn the motions.*

Communion Song:

As we come forward to the table of the Lord let us sing **"God Is So Good."** (Carey Landry, *Young People's Glory and Praise*, OCP.)

Concluding Rite

Closing Song:

We go forth as people of prayer singing our closing song, **"The Peace of the Lord."** (Gary Ault, *Young People's Glory and Praise*, OCP.)

Closing Procession:

The children who carried in the cross and children's lectionary now carry them out, accompanying the presider, as the closing song is sung.

 Cross   Children's lectionary

Our Father with Gestures

Hand gestures to the Our Father help children better understand the meaning of this prayer. The gestures can be led by the teacher or another adult. The children follow the teacher's lead in doing the motions as they sing or recite this prayer. The following gestures can be used:

Our Father	(arms outstretched)
Who art in heaven	(arms raised over head)
Hallowed be thy name.	(head bowed, hands folded)
Thy kingdom come,	(raise right arm)
Thy will be done	(raise left arm)
On earth	(move hands apart)
As it is in heaven.	(arms raised over head)
Give us this day our daily bread,	(palms up in front of body)
And forgive us our trespasses,	(hands crossed over heart)
As we forgive those	(arms in front of body)
Who trespass against us.	(arms crossed over chest)
And lead us not into temptation	(push hands away from body)
But deliver us from evil.	(hands crossed before face)
Amen	(arms raised over head)

MaRch

TRUST IN GOD
SAINT JOSEPH (MARCH 19)

Welcome:

On this day we honor Saint Joseph. He took loving care of Mary and Jesus. Saint Joseph was a patient and just person who trusted God in all things. He was always faithful to what God asked of him. Saint Joseph is an example for all of us.

Introductory Rites

Gathering Song:

As we prepare to celebrate together, let us sing, "Beatitude People." (Kathy Coleman, *Young People's Glory and Praise, Volume Two*, OCP.)

Entrance Procession:

Two children accompany the presider, carrying in the cross and children's lectionary as the gathering song is sung.

  Cross   Children's lectionary

Glory to God:

"Glory to God." (Jeffrey Honore, *Young People's Glory and Praise, Volume Two*, OCP.)

Liturgy of the Word

First Reading:

(This reading tells us that one of David's sons will be king.)
   Child reads Samuel 7:4-5, 12-14, 16 is read by a child from the Lectionary for Masses with Children #272.

   A reading from the second book of Samuel . . .

Responsorial Psalm:

"Praise, Praise, Praise." (Julie Howard, *Sing for Joy*, LP.)

Gospel Acclamation:

"Lenten Gospel Acclamation I." (Carey Landry, *Young People's Glory and Praise, Volume Two*, OCP.)

Gospel:

(This story tells how the child Jesus is found in the Temple.)
  Presider reads Luke 2:41-51 from the Lectionary for Masses with Children #272, B.

A reading from the holy gospel according to Luke . . .

Homily Ideas:

What saint do we celebrate today? (Saint Joseph). **Who was Saint Joseph?** (Husband of Mary and foster father of Jesus.) **What kinds of things do fathers do for their children?** (Take care of them, work to provide food, teach them, love them.) **Joseph did all these things for the child Jesus. Joseph must have been a special person if God trusted Jesus with him.**

  Things were not always easy for Joseph, but he did what God asked. He is the patron saint of travelers. What are some places that Joseph went? (Bethlehem where Jesus was born, Egypt when king Herod wanted to hurt Jesus, Nazareth where the Holy Family lived, and Jerusalem where Jesus was found by Mary and Joseph in the Temple.) **Saint Joseph was always faithful to God, we should be like Saint Joseph and do God's will in our lives.**

Creed:

"We Believe in God." (Carey Landry, *Young People's Glory and Praise, Volume Two*, OCP.)

General Intercessions:

The prayers are read by five children, with the assembly responding.

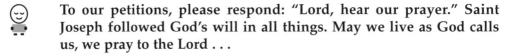 **To our petitions, please respond: "Lord, hear our prayer." Saint Joseph followed God's will in all things. May we live as God calls us, we pray to the Lord . . .**

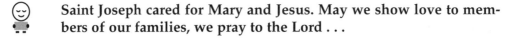 **Saint Joseph cared for Mary and Jesus. May we show love to members of our families, we pray to the Lord . . .**

Saint Joseph remained faithful to God despite hardships. May we trust God in all things, we pray to the Lord . . .

Saint Joseph was a patient teacher of the child Jesus. May we take time to share our talents with others, we pray to the Lord . . .

Saint Joseph was a model of a just person. May we be fair in our dealings with others, we pray to the Lord . . .

Liturgy of the Eucharist

Presentation Song:

As our gifts of bread and wine are brought forward, we praise God, singing "The Greatest Gift." (Carey Landry, *Young People's Glory and Praise, Volume Two,* OCP.)

Presentation of the Gifts:

As the song is sung, two children carry the gifts of bread and wine to the altar and hand them to the presider.

 Wine   Bread

Eucharistic Prayer:

Eucharistic Prayer for Masses with Children II.

Eucharistic Acclamations:

(Roc O'Connor, S.J. and Elizabeth Staehler, *Young People's Glory and Praise, Volume Two,* OCP.)

Communion Song:

Let us sing together our song during communion, "Receive Our Prayer." (Carey Landry, *Young People's Glory and Praise, Volume Two,* OCP.)

Concluding Rite

Announcement:

After Mass, a Saint Joseph table with cookies and brownies will be set up in the parish hall. All proceeds will go to *name of local charity* to benefit the poor. (See end of liturgy for information.)

Closing Song:

As we go forth today to live as the people of God, let us sing "God Has Made Us a Family." (Carey Landry, *Young People's Glory and Praise, Volume Two*, OCP.)

Closing Procession:

The children who carried in the cross and children's lectionary now carry them out, accompanying the presider, as the closing song is sung.

 Cross   Children's lectionary

Saint Joseph's Table

A long-time custom for celebrating this day is the Saint Joseph's table. Food is brought and shared and a collection is taken for the poor.

Children can adapt this custom by baking cookies, brownies, and other treats at home with their parents and donating them to the Saint Joseph's table.

The bakery table is set up before Mass in an area such as the parish hall. An offering box is placed on the table. A blessing is said with all those involved in this project participating. This blessing for the Saint Joseph's table can be found in the *Book of Blessings*. It includes intercessions, a litany, scripture reading and prayer in honor of the memory of Saint Joseph.

After Mass students, teachers, staff members, and parents make a monetary offering for each item. Let all the children know about the project ahead of time so that they can bring money if they wish to do so.

All the money donated is then given to a local charity that benefits the poor. This idea is in keeping with the season of Lent when we pray and give to others.

GOD IS GOOD
4TH SUNDAY IN LENT (B)

Welcome:

During this season of Lent, we come together to remember how much God loves us and all that God has done for us. A basket of crosses made by some of the children will be carried in the entrance procession as a sign that the children will walk with Jesus. (See end of liturgy for information on crosses.)

Introductory Rites

Gathering Song:

Our gathering song is "Jesus, Come to Us." (David Haas, *Rise Up and Sing,* OCP.)

Entrance Procession:

Two children accompany the presider, carrying in the cross, children's lectionary, and basket of paper crosses as the gathering song is sung.

 Cross   Basket of crosses   Children's lectionary

Penitential Rite:

During the season of Lent, we are called to change our hearts. Let us pause and remember the times we have not lived up to our baptismal promises.

For the times we were selfish and turned away from God,
   Lord, have mercy.
For the times we did not share what we had with others,
   Christ, have mercy.
For the times we hurt other people by our words or actions,
   Lord, have mercy.

Liturgy of the Word

First Reading:

(This reading reminds us that we are made alive in Christ.)

Two children read Ephesians 2:4-10 from the Lectionary for Masses with Children #28.

 A reading from the letter of Paul to the Ephesians . . . what Christ Jesus has done.

 You were saved . . . The word of the Lord.

Responsorial Psalm:

"Hear My Voice." (Julie Howard, *Sing for Joy*, LP.)

Gospel Acclamation:

"Praise to You, Lord Jesus Christ." (Owen Alstott, *Rise Up and Sing*, OCP.)

Gospel:

(This gospel proclaims that God loves us so much that the Son was sent to us.)

Presider reads John 3:16-17 from the Lectionary for Masses with Children #28.

A reading from the holy gospel according to John . . .

Homily Ideas:

During the season of Lent we recall the promises made for us at baptism. We are to reject sin and believe in God.

We must look at our lives and see what it is that keeps us from loving God and following Jesus with our whole heart. It may be concern with possessions or with what others think of us. We are to put aside whatever it is and make room in our hearts for the God who created us and loves us always. We are challenged to live as Jesus showed us.

Creed:

"We Believe in God." (Frank Alleruzzo, *Rise Up and Sing*, OCP.)

General Intercessions:

The prayers are read by five children, with the assembly responding.

During Lent, we are called to follow the way of Jesus. To our petitions, please respond: "Lord, hear our prayer." May we be people of love, helping others in the name of Jesus, we pray to the Lord . . .

 May we be people of compassion, reaching out to those in need, we pray to the Lord . . .

 May we be people of courage, following the way of Jesus each day, we pray to the Lord . . .

 May we be people of justice, working for the good of all people, we pray to the Lord . . .

 May we be people of faith, living the promises of baptism during Lent and always, we pray to the Lord . . .

Liturgy of the Eucharist

Presentation Song:

As the gifts are brought forward and the table is prepared, we sing together **"Forgiveness Prayer."** (Regina Pirruccello, *Rise Up and Sing*, OCP.)

Presentation of the Gifts:

As the song is sung, two children carry the gifts of bread and wine to the altar and hand them to the presider.

 Wine   Bread

Eucharistic Prayer and Acclamations:

"Eucharistic Prayer for Masses with Children II." (Christopher Walker, *Rise Up and Sing*, OCP.)

Lamb of God:

"Lamb of God." (Owen Alstott, *Rise Up and Sing*, OCP.)

Communion Song:

As we come forward to the table of the Lord, we sing together "You Call Us to Live." (Christopher Walker, *Rise Up and Sing*, OCP.)

Concluding Rite

Closing Song:

As we go forth to follow Jesus, we sing together "God Has Chosen Me."
(Bernadette Farrell, *Rise Up and Sing,* OCP.)

Closing Procession:

The children who carried in the cross and children's lectionary now carry them out, accompanying the presider, as the closing song is sung.

 Cross   Children's lectionary

Lenten Cross

During the week before the liturgy, talk with the children about following Jesus in their lives. Explain that we are to walk with Jesus during Lent and always.

As a sign that they will follow Jesus, ask each of the children to cut out a cross that has been duplicated on purple copy paper.

Before class make the crosses bearing the words: "I will walk with Jesus." Also provide a place for the individual child's name. (See. p. 199 for a reproducible Lenten cross model.) Ask the children to write their name on their cross as a sign that they will walk with Jesus.

All the crosses are collected in a basket and carried in the entrance procession. The basket is placed in front of the processional cross as a sign of our unity with Jesus Christ.

A MODEL OF FAITH
ANNUNCIATION OF THE LORD (MARCH 25)

Welcome:

We gather together today to celebrate the Annunciation of the Lord. We praise God for all that God has done for us through Mary. We too are to be open to the Holy Spirit at work in our lives.

Introductory Rites

Gathering Song:

Please stand and join in our gathering song, "Sing of Mary, Pure and Lowly." (*Hymnal for Catholic Students*, GIA.)

Entrance Procession:

Two children accompany the presider, carrying in the cross and children's lectionary as the gathering song is sung.

 Cross   Children's lectionary

Glory to God:

"Gloria." (Carroll T. Andrews, *Hymnal for Catholic Students*, GIA.)

Liturgy of the Word

First Reading:

(In this reading from Romans we hear that the good news is about Jesus Christ.)

   Romans 1:1-4 is read by a child from the Lectionary for Masses with Children #274.

 Our first reading is from the letter of Paul to the Romans . . .

Responsorial Psalm:

"Praise, Praise, Praise." (Julie Howard, *Sing for Joy*, LP.)

Gospel Acclamation:

"For Lent." (Frank Schoen, *Hymnal for Catholic Students*, GIA.)

Gospel:

(This gospel recounts how the angel Gabriel was sent to Mary.)
   Presider reads Luke 1:26-38 from the Lectionary for Masses with Children #274.
A reading from the holy gospel according to Luke . . .

Homily Ideas:

In the gospel story we hear how God sent the angel Gabriel to Mary to ask her to be the mother of Jesus. Mary said yes to God. She was open to the word of God in her life. We too are to say yes to what God asks in our lives.

What prayer do we say today that has the words of the angel in this gospel story? (Hail Mary.) Through this prayer we ask Mary to pray for us and with us to God.

We celebrate today because God has done great things for us through Mary. God loves us with an unending love.

General Intercessions:

The prayers are read by five children, with the assembly responding.

 To our petitions, please respond: "Lord, hear our prayer." Mary said yes to God. May we say yes to what God asks of us, we pray to the Lord . . .

 Mary served God all her life. May we serve God in all we do, we pray to the Lord . . .

 Mary gave her heart totally to God. May we show our love for God in all we do, we pray to the Lord . . .

 Mary had faith in God always. May we have faith even when times are difficult, we pray to the Lord . . .

 Mary praised God for his presence in her life. May we give glory and thanks to God for all his blessings, we pray to the Lord . . .

Liturgy of the Eucharist

Presentation Song:

The song during the presentation of the gifts today is "Canticle of Mary." (*Hymnal for Catholic Students*, GIA.)

Presentation of the Gifts:

As the song is sung, two children carry the gifts of bread and wine to the altar and hand them to the presider.

 Wine Bread

Eucharistic Prayer:

Eucharistic Prayer for Masses with Children II.

Eucharistic Acclamations:

"Mass of Creation." (Marty Haugen, *Hymnal for Catholic Students*, GIA.)

Communion Song:

As we come to the table of the Lord, join in our communion song, "I Am the Bread of Life." (Suzanne Toolan, *Hymnal for Catholic Students*, GIA.)

Concluding Rite

Announcement:

As you leave today, everyone is invited to take a Hail Mary prayer card from the baskets at the exits and pray this prayer at home. (See end of liturgy for information.)

Closing Song:

Our closing song is a traditional favorite to honor Mary. Join in singing "Immaculate Mary." (*Hymnal for Catholic Students*, GIA.)

Closing Procession:

The children who carried in the cross and children's lectionary now carry them out, accompanying the presider, as the closing song is sung.

 Cross Children's lectionary

Hail Mary Prayer Card

The words of the angel Gabriel and of Elizabeth in Luke's gospel are repeated in the traditional Hail Mary. This prayer has been prayed by generations of Christians to celebrate Mary and her role in our salvation. Make "Hail Mary prayer cards" for the children to take home after the liturgy bearing this important prayer. This will encourage the children to pray this prayer at home to honor Mary as the Mother of God and ask her prayers on our behalf.

To assemble these children's prayer cards, type a copy of the prayer and add clip art such as a flower or illustration of Mary. (See p. 200 for a reproducible copy of the Hail Mary.) Four cards can be copied at a time on a standard sheet of card stock. Blue should be used, as it is a traditional color for Mary. Cut the cards apart on a paper cutter for a clean edge.

Place the prayer cards in baskets at the exits of the church for the children to take home as a reminder and a call to pray.

HOSANNA!
PASSION SUNDAY (A)

Welcome:

This is Passion Sunday. We celebrate the entrance of Jesus into Jerusalem as the people shouted "Hosanna!" As a church, we enter into the holiest week of the church year. We journey with Jesus to the cross and resurrection.

Introductory Rites

Gathering Song:

Our gathering song today is "The King of Glory." (Rev. W.F. Jabusch, *Young People's Glory and Praise*, OCP.)

Entrance Procession:

All the children are given palms before Mass to wave during the entrance procession. Three children accompany the presider, carrying in the cross, children's lectionary, and a banner as the gathering song is sung. Three other children carry palms in the procession and then return to their places. (See description of banner at end of liturgy.)

 Cross   Children's lectionary   Banner

      Palms

Blessing of Palms:

Blessing of Palms (from *The Sacramentary*). *Children hold palms high as they are blessed.*

Liturgy of the Word

Opening Gospel:

(This gospel recounts how Jesus is hailed on entering Jerusalem.)
 Presider proclaims Matthew 21:1-11 from the Lectionary for Masses with Children #33.
A reading from the holy gospel according to Matthew . . .

Homily Ideas:

Why do we have palms today? (To help us celebrate when Jesus came into Jerusalem and people waved palms and shouted hosanna.)

What today is called? (Passion Sunday.) **What week is beginning?** (Holy Week.) **What do we experience during this week?** (Jesus' death on a cross and resurrection.) **Why did Jesus die and rise again?** (So we could have new life with God.)

First Reading:

(Isaiah tells how we should refuse to give up.)

Child reads Isaiah 50:6-7 from the Lectionary for Masses with Children #33.

 A reading from the book of the prophet Isaiah . . .

Gospel Acclamation:

"Lenten Gospel Acclamation." (Joe Regan, *Young People's Glory and Praise,* OCP.)

Gospel:

The passion account in Matthew 27:11-54 is proclaimed by the presider from the Lectionary for Masses with Children #33.

The passion of our Lord Jesus Christ according to Matthew . . .

General Intercessions:

The prayers are read by five children, with the assembly responding.

 To our petitions, please respond: "Lord, hear our prayer." That our journey to the cross with Jesus may help us to understand that God loves us with an unending love, we pray to the Lord . . .

 That we may follow Jesus in all things no matter what the cost, we pray to the Lord . . .

 That those who are ill in mind or body may find strength and healing, we pray to the Lord . . .

 That victims of prejudice and discrimination may know that they have hope in Jesus, we pray to the Lord . . .

 That our holy week experience may help us lead better lives, we pray to the Lord . . .

Liturgy of the Eucharist

Presentation Song:

Our song during the presentation of the gifts is "Peace Time." (Carey Landry, *Young People's Glory and Praise*, OCP.)

Presentation of the Gifts:

As the song is sung, two children carry the gifts of bread and wine to the altar and hand them to the presider.

 Wine  Bread

Eucharistic Prayer:

Eucharistic Prayer for Masses with Children II.

Eucharistic Acclamations:

"Acclamations for Prayer II." (Carey Landry, *Young People's Glory and Praise*, OCP.)

Communion Song:

Our song during communion today is "Be Not Afraid." (Bob Dufford, S.J., *Young People's Glory and Praise*, OCP.)

Concluding Rite

Closing Song:

Our song as we leave today to continue our Holy Week journey is "Only a Shadow." (Carey Landry, *Young People's Glory and Praise*, OCP.)

Closing Procession:

The children who carried in the cross and children's lectionary now carry them out, accompanying the presider, as the closing song is sung.

 Cross Children's lectionary

Processional Banner

A felt banner can be made for a student to carry in the entrance procession for the Passion Sunday liturgy. Use one yard of red felt for the banner background. Since felt comes in a very wide width, turn the felt sideways. Cut off about two feet from the top and sew a rod pocket. This makes a banner three feet wide by four feet long.

Enlarge letter patterns on p. 201 to cut out seven-inch high letters from gold felt to spell out "H-O-S-A-N-N-A." Then cut out two sixteen-inch palm branches from green felt. (Also see p. 201 for palm branch shape.) Lay out the banner decorations with the letters going down the banner and one palm branch on each side. Then attach the letters and palms to the banner with craft glue.

Slip a dowel rod through the rod pocket at the top. Then use a length of gold drapery cord with tassels to hang the banner. Tie the cord to either end of the rod. Hang the banner from a wood pole with a groove in the top to hold the cord in place.

At the beginning of the liturgy, an older student carries the banner leading the entrance procession to the altar. Then this student steps to the side of the altar and places the banner in the stand.

APRIL

NEW LIFE
WEEKDAY IN EASTER

Welcome:

We gather together today to celebrate the Easter season. We are an Easter people and a people of hope because of Jesus. A basket of "butterflies" made by each of the children will be brought forward during the entrance procession as a sign that all of us have new life through the resurrection of Jesus Christ. (See end of liturgy for description of butterflies.)

Introductory Rites

Gathering Song:

Give glory to God as we sing together our gathering song, "Rejoice! He Lives!" (Paul Coates and Timothy Crowley, *Young People's Glory and Praise, Volume Two*, OCP.)

Entrance Procession:

Three children accompany the presider, carrying in the cross, children's lectionary, and basket of butterflies as the gathering song is sung.

 Cross   Children's lectionary   Basket of butterflies

Glory to God:

"Glory to God." (Jeffrey Honore, *Young People's Glory and Praise, Volume Two*, OCP.)

Liturgy of the Word

First Reading:

(This reading tells us that God has raised Jesus to life.)
   Child reads Acts 2:32-33 from the Lectionary for Masses with Children #185.

    A reading from the Acts of the Apostles . . .

Responsorial Psalm:

"Come with Joy." (Julie Howard, *Sing for Joy*, LP.)

Gospel Acclamation:

"A Celebrational Alleluia." (Carey Landry, *Young People's Glory and Praise, Volume Two*, OCP.)

Gospel:

(This gospel tells how Mary Magdalene saw Jesus outside the tomb.)
    Presider proclaims John 20:11-18 from the Lectionary for Masses with Children #185.
A reading from the holy gospel according to John . . .

Homily Ideas:

All around us at Mass today we see signs of the new life Jesus Christ brings to us at Easter. The butterfly on the Easter banner reminds us that as the butterfly is changed inside the cocoon, so Jesus was transformed through the resurrection.

    The Easter lilies that decorate the altar steps are a sign of new life too. The Easter lily blooms from a dark bulb planted in the ground. Jesus too died, was placed in a tomb, and rose to glorious new life.

    The holy water we used to bless ourselves as we entered the church reminds us of our baptism in the name of Jesus Christ. As new members were baptized at the Easter Vigil, so we too are to live our baptismal promises. We are to grow in faith, hope, and love during this Easter season.

    The paschal candle is lit today and will remain lit throughout the Easter season. It is a sign that the risen Christ is here with us. Jesus is the light of our lives and we are to follow that light.

    In the new life of spring, the budding trees, the blooming flowers, we are reminded of the new life we have in Jesus. In our hearts we are reborn through the life, death, and resurrection of Jesus Christ. We are an Easter people. We are filled with joy and hope because of all God has done for us. Alleluia!

General Intercessions:

The prayers are read by five children, with the assembly responding.

 To our petitions, please respond: "Lord, hear our prayer." May the new life of spring remind us to thank God for the new life we have through Jesus Christ, we pray to the Lord . . .

May we be people of joy and hope always because of Easter, we pray to the Lord . . .

 May all people in all nations come to know the good news about Jesus Christ, we pray to the Lord . . .

 May we reach out to those who are suffering or in need during this Easter season, we pray to the Lord . . .

 May we live in love in the name of the risen Christ, we pray to the Lord . . .

Liturgy of the Eucharist

Presentation Song:

Our song as the table is prepared and the gifts are brought forward is "At the Table of Jesus." (Carey Landry, *Young People's Glory and Praise, Volume Two*, OCP.)

Presentation of the Gifts:

As the song is sung, two children carry the gifts of bread and wine to the altar and hand them to the presider.

 Wine   Bread

Eucharistic Prayer:

Eucharistic Prayer for Masses with Children III (using Easter inserts).

Eucharistic Acclamations:

(Roc O'Connor, S.J. and Elizabeth Staehler, *Young People's Glory and Praise, Volume Two*, OCP.)

Communion Song:

As we come forward to receive Jesus, our risen Savior, let us sing "Communion Hymn." (Carey Landry, *Young People's Glory and Praise, Volume Two*, OCP.)

Concluding Rite

Closing Song:

As we go to live as Easter people, we sing out "Alleluia, Praise You, Lord."
(Larry Folk, *Young People's Glory and Praise, Volume Two*, OCP.)

Closing Procession:

The children who carried in the cross and children's lectionary now carry them out, accompanying the presider, as the closing song is sung.

 Cross   Children's lectionary

New-Life Butterfly

Children can make individual paper butterflies the week before this liturgy as a reminder that all of us have new life in Jesus Christ. This activity encourages children to feel that they are a part of the Easter season liturgy.

A good size for a butterfly is 5" in diameter. Use a copy machine to duplicate sheets with outlines of butterflies on brightly colored paper. (See p. 202 for a reproducible butterfly shape.) Ask each child to cut out one of the butterflies. They can decorate their butterflies anyway they wish with designs and colorful markers.

The children should write their name on their butterflies. Then they may bend the butterflies in half in the middle for a three-dimensional look.

The colorful butterflies are placed in a large wicker basket to be carried in the entrance procession. The basket is placed in front of the cross as a reminder of the resurrection.

ALLELUIA!
2ND SUNDAY IN EASTER (C)

Welcome:

We are now celebrating the glorious season of Easter. This is a time of hope, a time of joy, and a time of new life. The risen Christ is with all of us. We are to have faith in God in everything we do.

Introductory Rites

Gathering Song:

Stand and sing out "Alleluia, Jesus Is Risen." (Joe Pinson, *Young People's Glory and Praise, Volume Two,* OCP.)

Entrance Procession:

Two children accompany the presider, carrying in the cross and children's lectionary as the gathering song is sung.

 Cross   Children's lectionary

Glory to God:

"Glory to God." (Jeffrey Honore, *Young People's Glory and Praise, Volume Two,* OCP.)

Liturgy of the Word

First Reading:

(This reading tells how the apostles worked miracles.) *Child reads Acts 5:12-16 from the* Lectionary for Masses with Children #39.

 A reading from the Acts of the Apostles . . .

Responsorial Psalm:

"Alleluia." (Carey Landry, *Young People's Glory and Praise, Volume Two,* OCP.)
    Psalm 118:2 and 4, 13-14 is read by children from the Lectionary for Masses with Children #39.

Let Israel . . . "God is always merciful!"

 The nations . . . he has saved me.

Gospel Acclamation:

"A Celebrational Alleluia." (Carey Landry, *Young People's Glory and Praise, Volume Two*, OCP.)

Gospel:

(This gospel is the story of Thomas.)
Presider proclaims John 20:19-29 from the Lectionary for Masses with Children #39.
A reading from the holy gospel according to John . . .

Homily Ideas:

What season are we celebrating? (Easter.) **How long does this season last?** (Fifty days.) **What are we celebrating during the Easter season?** (The resurrection of Jesus Christ and the new life we have because of Jesus.)

The paschal candle is lit for Mass today. What does it represent? (The risen Christ present with us.) **How long will it stay lit?** (For every Mass during the fifty days of the Easter season.)

In today's gospel we heard the story about one of the apostles. What was his name? (Thomas.) **Did Thomas believe that Jesus had risen from the dead?** (Not at first.) **When did he believe?** (After he saw Jesus.) **What did Thomas say to Jesus?** ("My Lord and my God.") **We too must believe in Jesus and live the gospel. How can we show faith in Jesus?** (Pray, help others, receive the eucharist.)

Creed:

"We Believe in God." (Carey Landry, *Young People's Glory and Praise, Volume Two*, OCP.)

General Intercessions:

The prayers are read by five children, with the assembly responding.

 To our petitions, please respond: "Lord, hear our prayer." May we follow the risen Christ in our lives by all we say and do, we pray to the Lord . . .

 May all people know the hope that comes to us through the resurrection of Jesus Christ, we pray to the Lord . . .

May the people baptized at the Easter Vigil continue to have our support and prayers, we pray to the Lord . . .

 May we continue to grow in faith, hope and love of God and others during the Easter season, we pray to the Lord . . .

 May we live as an Easter people, sharing the good news with others, we pray to the Lord . . .

Liturgy of the Eucharist

Presentation Song:

Our song today as the gifts are brought forward to the altar is "A Gift from Your Children." (Nancy Bourassa and Carey Landry, *Young People's Glory and Praise, Volume Two,* OCP.)

Presentation of the Gifts:

As the song is sung, two children carry the gifts of bread and wine to the altar and hand them to the presider.

 Wine   Bread

Eucharistic Prayer:

Eucharistic Prayer for Masses with Children III (using Easter inserts).

Eucharistic Acclamations:

(Roc O'Connor, S.J. and Elizabeth Staehler, *Young People's Glory and Praise, Volume Two,* OCP.)

Communion Song:

As people of hope join together in our Communion song, "At the Table of Jesus." (Carey Landry, *Young People's Glory and Praise, Volume Two,* OCP.)

Communion Meditation:

One of the classes will now present an Easter season reflection for us.
   Children come forward with letter cards spelling "A-L-L-E-L-U-I-A." (See script at end of liturgy.)

Concluding Rite

Solemn Blessing:

Solemn Blessing for the Easter season (from *The Sacramentary*.)

Closing Song:

As we go forth today to live the gospel, let us sing "Easter People." (David Light, *Young People's Glory and Praise, Volume Two*, OCP.)

Closing Procession:

The children who carried in the cross and children's lectionary now carry them out, accompanying the presider, as the closing song is sung.

 Cross   Children's lectionary

Alleluia Reflection

Children may participate in a meditation after Communion to help remind us of what the Easter season means. The reflection is announced by the prayer leader or teacher. Eight children come forward. Each child holds a large card, each with a letter printed on it so that they spell out the word "A-L-L-E-L-U-I-A." The children read statements off the back of the card as follows:

    A   is for all of us because Jesus was sent by the Father to all of us.

    L   is for life because Jesus brings us new life.

    L   is for love because we are to love others in the name of Jesus.

    E   is for the Easter season when we celebrate the resurrection of Jesus Christ.

    L   is for Lord because Jesus is our Lord and Savior.

    U   is for united because in Jesus we are united with God and one another.

    I   is for infinite because God loves each of us with an infinite love.

    A   is for alleluia because Jesus is with us always.

To assure visibility for both the congregation and the young reader, each card should be at least 12″ x 12″, with each letter being at least 9″ tall. The lettering for the reflection on the back of each card should be printed so as to facilitate ease of reading.

When each child has read his or her meditation, all the children say together "Alleluia, alleluia, alleluia!" The children then return to their places in the assembly for the blessing. The reflections help all of us to go forth to live as Easter people.

ROAD TO EMMAUS
3RD SUNDAY IN EASTER (A)

Welcome:

We celebrate the presence of the risen Christ among us. As Jesus was with the disciples on the road to Emmaus, so Jesus is with us through the eucharist. A basket of Easter pledges made by some of the children will be carried in the entrance procession as a reminder to live as Easter people. (See end of liturgy for instructions for Easter pledges.)

Introductory Rites

Gathering Song:

Our gathering song during this Easter season is "Easter People." (David Light, *Rise Up and Sing*, OCP.)

Entrance Procession:

Three children accompany the presider, carrying in the cross, children's lectionary, and basket of Easter pledges as the gathering song is sung.

 Cross   Children's lectionary   Basket of Easter pledges

Glory to God:

"Glory to God." (Michael Lynch, *Rise Up and Sing*, OCP.)

Liturgy of the Word

First Reading:

(This reading tells how Peter told that crowd that God raised Jesus from death to life.)

Child reads Acts 2:14,22-24 from the Lectionary for Masses with Children #40.

 A reading from the Acts of the Apostles . . .

Responsorial Psalm:

"Alleluia." (Carey Landry, *Rise Up and Sing*, OCP.)

Children read Psalm 118:1-2,46, 50 from the Lectionary for Masses with Children #40.

 I love you . . . and my place of shelter.

 You are . . . to your chosen king.

Gospel Acclamation:

"Alleluia, Shout with Joy." (Barbara Bridge and Dominic MacAller, *Rise Up and Sing*, OCP.)

Gospel:

(This gospel tells the story of the risen Christ and the disciples on the road to Emmaus.)

The presider reads Luke 24:13-35 from the Lectionary for Masses with Children #40.

A reading from the holy gospel according to Luke . . .

Homily Ideas:

We are on a journey of faith like the disciples in the gospel story today. We do not always recognize Jesus at work in our lives. The disciples in the gospel finally recognized Jesus through scripture and the breaking of bread. Jesus Christ is here with us too in his word and in the eucharist.

Creed:

"We Believe." (Christopher Walker, *Rise Up and Sing*, OCP.)

General Intercessions:

The prayers are read by five children, with the assembly responding.

 To our petitions, please respond: "Lord, hear our prayer." May we recognize the risen Christ who is with us on our journey to the Father, we pray to the Lord . . .

 May we remember that Jesus Christ is the way, the truth, and the life, we pray to the Lord . . .

 May the Easter experience help us to become all that God created us to be, we pray to the Lord . . .

May we live always as a community of God's people believing in the power of the gospel, we pray to the Lord . . .

 May all of us who celebrate the Eucharist together today take Christ with us to all we meet, we pray to the Lord . . .

Liturgy of the Eucharist

Presentation Song:

Join in our song as the bread and wine are brought forward, "Jesus, You Love Us." (Christopher Walker, *Rise Up and Sing*, OCP.)

Presentation of the Gifts:

As the song is sung, two children carry the gifts of bread and wine to the altar and hand them to the presider.

 Wine   Bread

Eucharistic Prayer:

Eucharistic Prayer for Masses with Children III (using Easter inserts).

Eucharistic Acclamations:

(Dominic MacAller, *Rise Up and Sing*, OCP.)

Communion Song:

As we share the eucharist together, let us sing "You Are My Hope." (Marie-Jo Thum, *Rise Up and Sing*, OCP.)

Concluding Rite

Closing Song:

As we go out today, we lift our voices and hearts in song as we sing together "Living Is the Word." (Monica Brown, *Rise Up and Sing*, OCP.)

Closing Procession:

The children who carried in the cross and children's lectionary now carry them out, accompanying the presider, as the closing song is sung.

 Cross   Children's lectionary

Easter People Pledge

We are an Easter people because of Jesus Christ. We are to live the spirit of the Easter season. One week before the Easter liturgy, encourage the students to think of things they can do to make the world a better place for all people. Discuss various ways this might be done such as praying for others, inviting people to church, being kind to others, telling other people about God's love, and sharing with those in need.

Then ask the children to fill out an "Easter People Pledge." A half sheet is needed for each student. The pledge states: "As a person who has new life in Jesus Christ I will do the following to make the world a better place. . . . " Provide two lines on which the students can write what they will do. Also provide a place for them to sign their name. (See p. 203 for a reproducible Easter People Pledge form.)

Be sure to stress that what is written on the pledge should be something that the individual student is prepared to carry out during the coming weeks of the Easter season. Remind the students that we can do all things in Jesus Christ.

The children roll up their pledges and tie them with green yarn. The pledges are then carried in a basket in the entrance procession as a sign that we are an Easter people who will live as Jesus showed us.

ONE IN JESUS
WEEKDAY IN EASTER

Welcome:

We come together during this Easter season to remember that we are one with one another in Jesus. The message of Jesus Christ should shine in our hearts and our lives.

Introductory Rites

Gathering Song:

Stand and sing praise to God through our gathering song, "New Hope." (Carey Landry, *Young People's Glory and Praise*, OCP.)

Entrance Procession:

Two children accompany the presider, carrying in the cross and children's lectionary as the gathering song is sung.

 Cross   Children's lectionary

Liturgy of the Word

First Reading:

(In this reading we hear how the followers of Jesus shared everything they had with each other.)

　　Child reads Acts 4:32-35 from the Lectionary for Masses with Children #187.

　　A reading from the Acts of the Apostles . . .

Responsorial Psalm:

"Come with Joy." (Julie Howard, *Sing for Joy*, LP.)

Gospel Acclamation:

"Alleluia." (Donald J. Reagan, *Young People's Glory and Praise*, OCP.)

Gospel:

(In this gospel Jesus prays to God that his followers be one with each other.)
Presider reads John 17:21-23 from the Lectionary for Masses with Children #187.
A reading from the holy gospel according to John . . .

Homily Ideas:

In the first reading we see that in the early church the followers of Jesus shared everything they had with each other and also shared the good news of Jesus' resurrection. This is how we should live as a church today.

The gospel tells us that Jesus prayed to God that all of us would be one with one another as Jesus Christ is one with the Father and the Holy Spirit. As a community of God's people, we share in the love and unity of the Trinity. It is important to remember that as an Easter people we are on this faith journey together.

General Intercessions:

The prayers are read by five children, with the assembly responding.

 To our petitions, please respond: "Lord, hear our prayer." May we tell people the good news about Jesus Christ, we pray to the Lord . . .

 May other people learn about God's love by the way we live our lives, we pray to the Lord . . .

 May our church work to meet the needs of all people, we pray to the Lord . . .

 May our lives give praise to God who created us and redeemed us, we pray to the Lord . . .

 May this Easter season be a time of new hope for all of us, we pray to the Lord . . .

Liturgy of the Eucharist

Presentation Song:

As the gifts are brought forward one of the children will carry a basket of meal tickets for people in need. (See information on meal tickets at end of liturgy.) **Our song during the presentation of the gifts is "This Is My Commandment."** *(Young People's Glory and Praise,* OCP.)

Presentation of the Gifts:

As the song is sung, three children carry the bread, wine, and basket of meal tickets to the altar. The bread and wine are handed to the presider, and the basket of meal tickets is placed at the base of the processional cross.

 Wine   Bread   Basket of meal tickets

Eucharistic Prayer:

Eucharistic Prayer for Masses with Children III (using Easter inserts).

Eucharistic Acclamations:

"Acclamations III." (Carey Landry, *Young People's Glory and Praise,* OCP.)

Communion Song:

Remembering all God has done for us, we will sing our Communion song, "His Banner Over Us Is Love." *(Young People's Glory and Praise,* OCP.)

Concluding Rite

Closing Song:

To the God who gives us life we sing out "Sing a New Song." (Dan Schutte, S.J., *Young People's Glory and Praise,* OCP.)

Closing Procession:

The children who carried in the cross and children's lectionary now carry them out, accompanying the presider, as the closing song is sung.

    Cross   Children's lectionary

Meal Ticket

In the readings for today's liturgy we see how the followers of Jesus shared with others. We too are to help others. One way to do this is by making a donation to a program that provides hot meals to people in need in the local community.

The students can be encouraged to earn money as a group by recycling or individually by doing chores at home. The money collected is then donated to this project. One way to track the contributions in a way the students can understand is with meal tickets.

These tickets can be made out of different colors of paper. Eight meal tickets can be made from each sheet of paper. On each piece should be the words "Meal Ticket" and "This ticket will provide one hot meal for a person in need in our community." Clip art can be used for illustration. (See p. 204 for a reproducible meal ticket form.)

Find out from the organization that provides the meals how much each meal costs to provide. Then each time a class has collected that much money, the children can put a meal ticket in a basket. Before the liturgy, collect all the meal tickets from all the classes and put them together in a basket to be carried in the gifts procession.

This project enables the children to reach out to people in need in their communities. The monetary contribution is then be forwarded to the sponsoring organization.

MAy

THE GOOD SHEPHERD
4TH SUNDAY IN EASTER (B)

Welcome:

Welcome to our liturgy. Today we celebrate that Jesus is the Good Shepherd who knows and cares for us. We are to hear Jesus' call in our lives. In the entrance procession sheep made by one of the classes will be brought forward as a sign of being willing to follow Jesus, the Good Shepherd.

Introductory Rites

Gathering Song:

Join in our gathering song, "Awake! Arise and Rejoice!" (Marie-Jo Thum, *Rise Up and Sing*, OCP).

Entrance Procession:

Three children accompany the presider, carrying in the cross, children's lectionary, and basket of "name sheep" as the gathering song is sung. (See end of liturgy for information.)

 Cross   Children's lectionary   Basket of name sheep

Glory to God:

"Glory to God." (Michael Lynch, *Rise Up and Sing*, OCP.)

Liturgy of the Word

First Reading:

(In this reading we are reminded that only Jesus has the power to save.)
  Two children read Acts 4:8-12 from the Lectionary for Masses with Children #44.

 A reading from the Acts of the Apostles . . . from Nazareth.

 You . . . The word of the Lord.

Responsorial Psalm:

"Alleluia" (Carey Landry, *Rise Up and Sing*, OCP.)
   Verses of Psalm 118:1, 21, 22-23) are read by children from the Lectionary for Masses with Children #44.

   Tell the LORD . . . and saving me.

   The stone . . . amazing to us.

Second Reading:

(In this reading we recall that we are God's children.)
   1 John 3:1-2 is read by children from the Lectionary for Masses with Children #44.

   A reading from the first letter of John . . . who we are.

   My dear friends . . . The word of the Lord.

Gospel Acclamation:

"Alleluia, Shout with Joy." (Barbara Bridge and Dominic MacAller, *Rise Up and Sing*, OCP.)

Gospel:

(The gospel reveals Jesus as the Good Shepherd.)
   John 10:11-16 is read by the presider from the Lectionary for Masses with Children #44.
A reading from the holy gospel of John . . .

Homily Ideas:

Have you ever been lost? (Yes.) **How did you feel?** (Scared.) **Who found you?** (Mom or Dad.) **How did you feel then?** (Happy.)
   In the gospel today we hear that Jesus says "I am the good shepherd." A shepherd is a person who takes care of a flock of sheep. A shepherd leads the sheep to green grass and water and keeps them safe. Jesus takes cares of us. We are the sheep who belong to Jesus. Jesus calls us and we should follow Jesus as the sheep follow the shepherd. We should listen to the voice of Jesus, the Good Shepherd, in our lives.

Creed:

"We Believe." (Christopher Walker, *Rise Up and Sing*, OCP.)

General Intercessions:

The prayers are read by five children, with the assembly responding.

 We pray for the needs of our church, our community, and our world. To our petitions, please respond: "Lord, hear our prayer." May we follow Jesus, the Good Shepherd, in all things, we pray to the Lord . . .

 May leaders of countries work for the good of all people, we pray to the Lord . . .

 May we reach out to those who feel lost or afraid, we pray to the Lord . . .

 May we always be welcomed back by Jesus when we stray, we pray to the Lord . . .

 May our church help all people to know the presence of the risen Christ in our lives, we pray to the Lord . . .

Liturgy of the Eucharist

Presentation Song:

As the table is prepared and our gifts are brought forward, please join in "Like a Shepherd." (Marianne Misetich, SNJM, *Rise Up and Sing,* OCP.)

Presentation of the Gifts:

As the song is sung, two children carry the gifts of bread and wine to the altar and hand them to the presider.

 Wine   Bread

Eucharistic Prayer:

Eucharistic Prayer for Masses with Children III (using Easter inserts).

Eucharistic Acclamations:

(Dominic MacAller, *Rise Up and Sing,* OCP.)

Communion Song:

During Communion time we will sing joyfully together "The King of Love My Shepherd Is" (*Rise Up and Sing,* OCP).

Concluding Rite

Closing Song:

As we go forth today to share the good news we sing together "Take the Word of God with You." (James Harrison and Christopher Walker, *Rise Up and Sing*, OCP.)

Closing Procession:

The children who carried in the cross and children's lectionary now carry them out, accompanying the presider as the closing song is sung.

 Cross   Children's lectionary

Name Sheep

The gospel for this liturgy reminds us that the Good Shepherd brings the sheep together. Students can make individual sheep with their names written on them as a sign they will follow Jesus, who is the Good Shepherd.

Each child should get a paper sheep on which is printed: "I will follow Jesus, the Good Shepherd." A line should also be provided for the student's signature. Use a copier to duplicate the sheep on p. 205 onto a half sheet of white paper for each student.

Ask the children to write their name on the line provided on the sheep as a pledge that they will follow Jesus, the Good Shepherd. The sheep are collected and carried in a basket in the opening procession by one of the children.

JESUS' PROMISE
ASCENSION THURSDAY (C)

Welcome:

We gather together to give praise and glory to God. Today we celebrate Ascension Thursday when Jesus returned to the Father. We are to live as people guided by the Holy Spirit in all things.

Introductory Rites

Gathering Song:

Sing out our gathering song, "Alleluia, Jesus Is Risen." (Joe Pinson, *Young People's Glory and Praise, Volume Two*, OCP.)

Entrance Procession:

Two children accompany the presider, carrying in the cross and children's lectionary as the gathering song is sung.

 Cross   Children's lectionary

Glory to God:

"Glory to God." (Jeffrey Honore, *Young People's Glory and Praise, Volume Two*, OCP.)

Liturgy of the Word

First Reading:

(In this reading we recall that Jesus told the disciples the Holy Spirit will come.)
   Acts 1:8-11 is read by three children from the Lectionary for Masses with Children #54.

 A reading from the Acts of the Apostles . . . in the world."

 After . . . into the sky.

 Suddenly . . . The word of the Lord.

May

Responsorial Psalm:

"God Mounts His Throne to Shouts of Joy." (Carey Landry, *Young People's Glory and Praise, Volume Two*, OCP.)

    Psalm 47:1-2, 5-6, 7-8 is read by children from the Lectionary for Masses with Children #54.

 All of you nations . . . ruler of all the earth.

 God goes up . . . God our King.

 God is ruler . . . from his sacred throne.

Second Reading:

(In this reading we are reminded that Christ rules over all.)

    Children read Ephesians 1:17-21 from the Lectionary for Masses with Children #54.

 A reading from the letter of Paul to the Ephesians . . . know God.

 My prayer . . . all of God's people.

 I want . . . The word of the Lord.

Gospel Acclamation:

"Alleluia." (Roc O'Connor, S.J., *Young People's Glory and Praise, Volume Two*, OCP.)

Gospel:

(This gospel proclaims that Jesus is taken up into heaven.)

    The presider proclaims Luke 24:50-53 from the Lectionary for Masses with Children #54.

A reading from the holy gospel according to Luke . . .

Homily Ideas:

Today is Ascension Thursday. We celebrate this holy day forty days after Easter. We remember that Jesus went to heaven in glory to be with the Father. Jesus is also still here with us through his Spirit of Love.

    Soon we will celebrate Pentecost. This is the day Jesus sent the Holy Spirit to the apostles. We too are to follow Jesus. The Holy Spirit will help us and guide us in all that we do.

Creed:

"We Believe in God." (Carey Landry, *Young People's Glory and Praise, Volume Two*, OCP.)

General Intercessions:

The prayers are read by five children, with the assembly responding.

To our petitions, please respond: "Lord, hear our prayer." That we may follow the teachings of Jesus Christ always, we pray to the Lord . . .

That we may praise the Father all for he has done for us through Jesus Christ, we pray to the Lord . . .

That all those who are ill, especially those in the hospital, may feel the healing presence of Christ, we pray to the Lord . . .

That during this holy Easter season we may take time for prayer and for one another, we pray to the Lord . . .

That all those who have died may live in God's peace forever, we pray to the Lord . . .

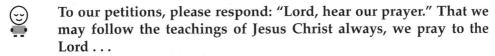

Liturgy of the Eucharist

Presentation Song:

Our offering for the home missions will be brought forward with the bread and wine. Our song during the presentation of the gifts is "Here Am I, O Lord." (Carey Landry, *Young People's Glory and Praise, Volume Two,* OCP.)

Presentation of the Gifts:

As the song is sung, three children carry the bread, wine, and donations for the home missions to the altar. The bread and wine are handed to the presider, and the donations are placed at the base of the processional cross. (See end of liturgy for information on mission collection.)

Bread   Wine   Mission collection

Eucharistic Prayer:

Eucharistic Prayer for Masses with Children III (using Easter inserts).

Eucharistic Acclamations:

(Roc O'Connor, S.J. and Elizabeth Staehler, *Young People's Glory and Praise, Volume Two*, OCP)

Communion Song:

Join in our song as we come to the table of the Lord, "Receive Our Prayer." (Carey Landry, *Young People's Glory and Praise, Volume Two*, OCP.)

Concluding Rite

Solemn Blessing:

Solemn Blessing for Ascension Thursday. (From *The Sacramentary*.)

Closing Song:

As we go forth, we sing praise to God. Our closing song is "Our God Is So Good." (Monica Brown, *Young People's Glory and Praise, Volume Two*, OCP.)

Closing Procession:

The children who carried in the cross and children's lectionary now carry them out, accompanying the presider as the closing song is sung.

 Cross   Children's lectionary

Home Missions Collection

The life, death, and resurrection of Jesus was for all people. We are to share the hope of the Easter season with others in Jesus' name. There are many small, isolated parishes who do not have money to purchase Bibles and other teaching materials for children to learn about Jesus Christ. Many families in these rural areas live in poverty and the Sunday collection is small. These home missions need our help.

Ask the children and families to donate to the Catholic Church Extension Society so that they can help poor parishes afford supplies for religious education for parish children. Place a marked collection basket on a table at the back of the church. Encourage children to bring in money they have earned to help other children in this way. The collection basket is brought forward in procession with the gifts of bread and wine.

Send a check for the money collected to the Catholic Extension Society at 35 East Wacker Drive, Chicago, IL 60601-2105. This is one way to be a disciple and bring the good news to others in the spirit of the Easter season.

FATHER, SON, AND SPIRIT
TRINITY SUNDAY (A)

Welcome:

This is Trinity Sunday. We remember that God is Father, Son, and Holy Spirit. We share in the divine life and love of the Trinity.

Introductory Rites

Gathering Song:

Sing out joyfully to God through our gathering song, "Into the House of God." (Carey Landry, *Young People's Glory and Praise, Volume Two*, OCP.)

Entrance Procession:

Two children accompany the presider, carrying in the cross and children's lectionary as the gathering song is sung.

 Cross   Children's lectionary

Glory to God:

"Glory to God." (Jeffrey Honore, *Young People's Glory and Praise, Volume Two*, OCP.)

Liturgy of the Word

First Reading:

(This reading recounts how the Lord told Moses, "I am the LORD.")
     Child reads Exodus 34:4-6, 8-9 from the Lectionary for Masses with Children #158.

 A reading from the book of Exodus . . .

Responsorial Psalm:

"A New Song." (*Sing for Joy*, LP.)

Second Reading:

(In this passage Paul prays that the Lord Jesus Christ will bless the people.)
Child reads from the Second Letter of Paul to the Corinthians 13:11-13 from the Lectionary for Masses with Children #158.

 A reading from the second letter of Paul to the Corinthians . . .

Gospel Acclamation:

"Alleluia." (Roc O'Connor, S.J., *Young People's Glory and Praise, Volume Two,* OCP.)

Gospel:

(This gospel reminds us that God gives us the only Son.)
Presider reads John 3:16-17 from the Lectionary for Masses with Children #158.
A reading from the holy gospel according to John . . .

Homily Ideas:

There are three persons in one God—Father, Son, and Holy Spirit. God our Father created us and our world. The Father sent the Son, Jesus Christ, to teach us and bring us new life through death and resurrection. Jesus sent the Holy Spirit to be with us and guide us. The Holy Spirit is in each of our hearts. We are to live as people of the Trinity.

Creed:

The Apostles' Creed will be said today in parts by the various grade levels. (See information at end of liturgy.)

General Intercessions:

The prayers are read by five children, with the assembly responding.

 To our petitions, please respond: "Lord, hear our prayer." That we give praise to the Father for all he has done for us, we pray to the Lord . . .

 That we live the commandments as Jesus Christ showed us, we pray to the Lord . . .

 That our hearts will be open to the Holy Spirit in our lives, we pray to the Lord . . .

That we live up to the promises made for us at baptism, we pray to the Lord . . .

 That the church throughout the world will proclaim the good news to all people, we pray to the Lord . . .

Liturgy of the Eucharist

Presentation Song:

Join in our song during the presentation of the gifts, "Spirit of Love." (David Light, *Young People's Glory and Praise, Volume Two*, OCP.)

Presentation of the Gifts:

As the song is sung, two children carry the gifts of bread and wine to the altar and hand them to the presider.

 Wine   Bread

Eucharistic Prayer:

Eucharistic Prayer for Masses with Children II.

Eucharistic Acclamations:

(Roc O'Connor, S.J. and Elizabeth Staehler, *Young People's Glory and Praise, Volume Two*, OCP.)

Communion Song:

Let us lift our voices in song to praise God by singing our communion song, "We Come to You." (Paul Coates and Timothy Crowley, *Young People's Glory and Praise, Volume Two*, OCP.)

Concluding Rite

Closing Song:

As we go forth to live as the people of the Trinity, let us sing together "Spirit of God, Come to Us." (Sr. Veronica McGrath and Carey Landry, *Young People's Glory and Praise, Volume Two*, OCP.)

Closing Procession:

The children who carried in the cross and children's lectionary now carry them out, accompanying the presider as the closing song is sung.

  Cross   Children's lectionary

Creed in Parts

Saying this creed in parts helps the students take a closer look at what we believe. Each grade level (or some other small group of children) can say a section of the Apostles' Creed. You may, of course, need to divide children in different ways depending upon the group with which you are working. If possible, distribute the text to the children ahead of time so that each group can say their part from memory. If that is not possible, distribute the text before the liturgy begins. (See p. 206 for a reproducible copy of the text of the creed.)

Apostles' Creed

1st group   **We believe in God, the Father Almighty,
Creator of heaven and earth.**

2nd group   **We believe in Jesus Christ, his only Son, Our Lord.
Who was conceived by the Holy Spirit
And born of the Virgin Mary.**

3rd group   **He suffered under Pontius Pilate,
Was crucified, died, and was buried.
He descended to the dead and
On the third day he rose again.**

4th group   **He ascended into heaven,
And is seated at the right hand of the Father.
He will come again to judge
The living and the dead.**

5th group   **We believe in the Holy Spirit,
The holy catholic Church,
The communion of saints,
The forgiveness of sins,
The resurrection of the body,
And life everlasting.**

All: **Amen.**

LOVE GOD AND OTHERS
WEEKDAY IN ORDINARY TIME

Welcome:

Our God is a God of love. We are called to love God and love others. We are to care about all people and share God's love with them. We are to be caring, compassionate people as Jesus showed us.

Introductory Rites

Gathering Song:

We gather together as the people of God and sing "Welcome to the Kingdom." (G.W. Hardin and Barbara Bridge, *Rise Up and Sing*, OCP.)

Entrance Procession:

Two children accompany the presider, carrying in the cross and children's lectionary as the gathering song is sung.

 Cross   Children's lectionary

Liturgy of the Word

First Reading:

(This reading reminds us that we must help other people.)

Child reads 1 John 3:11,18 from the Lectionary for Masses with Children #214.

 A reading from the first letter of John . . .

Responsorial Psalm:

"Protect Me, O God." (Julie Howard, *Sing for Joy*, LP.)

Gospel Acclamation:

"Alleluia, Shout with Joy." (Barbara Bridge and Dominic MacAller, *Rise Up and Sing*, OCP.)

Gospel:

(The gospel today is the greatest commandment and the story of the Good Samaritan.)

Presider proclaims Luke 10:25-37 from the Lectionary for Masses with Children #214.

A reading from the holy gospel according to Luke . . .

Homily Ideas:

What is the greatest commandment that Jesus taught us? (Love God and love others.) **The story of the Good Samaritan challenges us to consider all people our neighbors and treat all people with respect and kindness. We have many opportunities to help others. If there was a new child at school who didn't seem to fit in yet, how could you show kindness?** (Talk to the new child about their interests. Eat lunch with the new student. Introduce the new child to others students.)

If your friend's mom were ill in the hospital, what could you do? (Make a get well card. Talk to the friend about their feelings. Invite the friend to your house.)

If you saw on the news that people were going hungry in your town, how could you help? (Do chores and donate the money to the local soup kitchen. Pray for all those who go to bed hungry at night. Talk to your teacher and parents about starting a canned food drive in your school or neighborhood.)

Another way you can help other people is what you have done today. You have brought toys for children in the local children's hospital. Some of you brought puzzles, some brought games, others brought stuffed animals. Some of you are praying for the children who are ill. In this way we follow Jesus in helping others.

General Intercessions:

The prayers are read by five children, with the assembly responding.

 To our petitions, please respond: "Lord, hear our prayer." Jesus, you did the will of the Father. May we give praise to God through all we do, we pray to the Lord . . .

 Jesus, you showed us how to live as your followers. May we be witness to your word and example by the way we live, we pray to the Lord . . .

 Jesus, you helped others, especially those in need. May we reach out to all people, we pray to the Lord . . .

Jesus, you taught us to have compassion. May we care about others in your name, we pray to the Lord . . .

 Jesus, you showed us the Father's love. May we proclaim the good news to others, we pray to the Lord . . .

Liturgy of the Eucharist

Presentation Song:

Today some of the toys collected for the local children's hospital will be brought forward with the gifts of bread and wine. Our song during the presentation of the gifts is "Jesus, You Love Us." (Christopher Walker, *Rise Up and Sing*, OCP.)

Presentation of the Gifts:

As the song is sung, three children carry the bread, wine, and basket of toys collected for patients at the local children's hospital to the altar. The bread and wine are handed to the presider, and the basket of toys is placed at the base of the processional cross. (See end of liturgy for information on this project.)

 Basket of toys   Wine   Bread

Eucharistic Prayer and Acclamations:

"Eucharistic Prayer for Masses with Children II." (Christopher Walker, *Rise Up and Sing*, OCP.)

Communion Song:

As we share the eucharist together, we will sing our communion song, "Thank You Jesus." (Frank Alleruzzo, *Rise Up and Sing*, OCP.)

Concluding Rite

Closing Song:

We take the word of God with us, singing "Proclaim the Good News." (G.W. Hardin and Barbara Bridge, *Rise Up and Sing*, OCP.)

Closing Procession:

The children who carried in the cross and children's lectionary now carry them out, accompanying the presider, as the closing song is sung.

 Cross Children's lectionary

Hospital Collection

Well in advance of this liturgy, ask for donations of stuffed animals, books, and toys for the local children's hospital. (The reproducible letter on p. 207 can be duplicated and then sent home to families explaining this project.)

Place marked collection boxes at the back of the church. Bring some of the items forward in a large basket as part of the presentation of the gifts.

Index of Children's Liturgies

Index of Gospel Stories

Reproducible Section

The pages in this section are intended to be duplicated in conjunction with the liturgies in this book. Those who have purchased this book may feel free to copy them for use with these liturgies without permission from the publisher. They may not be copied by anyone else, or for any other purpose, without the written permission of the publisher.

Children's Liturgy Planning Form

Date: _____

Welcome:_____

Introductory Rites

Gathering Song: _____

Entrance Procession: _____

Penitential Rite: _____

Glory to God: _____

Liturgy of the Word

First Reading:_____

Responsorial Psalm: _____

Second Reading: _____

Gospel Acclamation: _____

Gospel: _____

Homily: _____

Creed:_____

General Intercessions: _____

Children's Liturgy Planning Form

Liturgy of the Eucharist

Closing Song: _____

Presentation Song: _____

Presentation of the Gifts: _____

Eucharistic Prayer: _____

Eucharistic Acclamations: _____

Our Father: _____

Communion Song: _____

Communion Meditation: _____

Concluding Rite

Announcement:_____

Closing Procession:_____

Preparation needed for craft or special activity:

_____

_____

_____

Notes:

_____

_____

_____

Children's Liturgy Participation

Date: _____

(Fill in names of children)

Cross: _____

Children's lectionary: _____

First reading: _____

_____

Responsorial psalm: _____

_____

Second reading: _____

General intercessions: _____

_____

_____

_____

_____

Presentation of the Gifts: _____

_____

General Intercessions

Date: _____

_____

_____,

we pray to the Lord . . .

_____

_____,

we pray to the Lord . . .

_____

_____,

we pray to the Lord . . .

_____

_____,

we pray to the Lord . . .

_____

_____,

we pray to the Lord . . .

Care Card I will show care
to others as Jesus teaches us by

_____

Signed

_____

Care Card I will show care
to others as Jesus teaches us by

_____

Signed

_____

Dear Families,

At the next children's liturgy, we will be celebrating the feast of Saint Vincent de Paul, a saint who distinguished himself by service to the poor and needy.

To help the children learn this same concern for others, we are collecting books to be donated to a homeless shelter. Please take the time to help your child find a suitable book to give. He or she may want to donate one of his or her own books that is still in good condition, or perhaps you will decide together to buy a new one.

Please have your child bring the book to the next children's liturgy. Thank you so much for your help.

Sincerely,

Dear Families,

At the next children's liturgy, we will be celebrating the feast of Saint Vincent de Paul, a saint who distinguished himself by service to the poor and needy.

To help the children learn this same concern for others, we are collecting books to be donated to a homeless shelter. Please take the time to help your child find a suitable book to give. He or she may want to donate one of his or her own books that is still in good condition, or perhaps you will decide together to buy a new one.

Please have your child bring the book to the next children's liturgy. Thank you so much for your help.

Sincerely,

My Peace Prayer

_____

_____

_____

_____

_____

Name _____

Peace I leave with you;
my peace I give to you (John 14:27)

My Peace Prayer

_____

_____

_____

_____

_____

Name _____

Peace I leave with you;
my peace I give to you (John 14:27)

Reproducible Section

Heart Cards

Jesus,
I will turn my heart and my life toward you.

_____
Name

Jesus,
I will turn my heart and my life toward you.

_____
Name

Stewardship Card

STEWARDSHIP CARD

GIVE FROM THE HEART

I will give to other people by:

_____

_____

_____

Signed, _____

STEWARDSHIP CARD

GIVE FROM THE HEART

I will give to other people by:

_____

_____

_____

Signed, _____

Reproducible Section

Faith

FAITH

Lenten Crosses

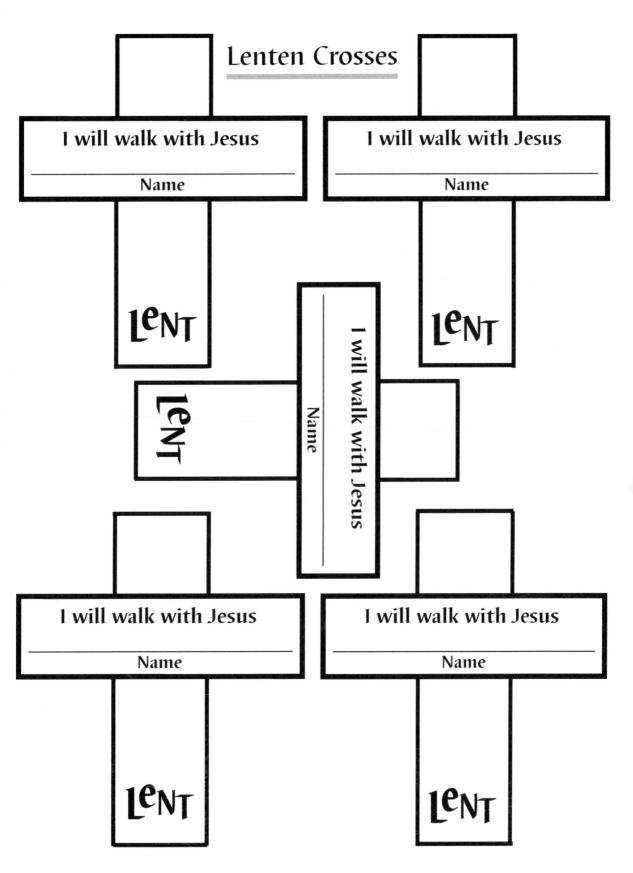

I will walk with Jesus

Name

I will walk with Jesus

Name

LENT

LENT

I will walk with Jesus

Name

LENT

I will walk with Jesus

Name

I will walk with Jesus

Name

LENT

LENT

Hail Mary Prayer Cards

Hail, Mary, full of grace,
the Lord is with you!
Blessed are you
 among women,
and Blessed is the fruit
 of your womb, Jesus.
Holy Mary, Mother of God,
pray for us sinners,
now and at the hour of
 our death. Amen.

Hail, Mary, full of grace,
the Lord is with you!
Blessed are you
 among women,
and Blessed is the fruit
 of your womb, Jesus.
Holy Mary, Mother of God,
pray for us sinners,
now and at the hour
 of our death. Amen.

Hail, Mary, full of grace,
the Lord is with you!
Blessed are you
 among women,
and Blessed is the fruit
 of your womb, Jesus.
Holy Mary, Mother of God,
pray for us sinners,
now and at the hour
 of our death. Amen.

Hail, Mary, full of grace,
the Lord is with you!
Blessed are you
 among women,
and Blessed is the fruit
 of your womb, Jesus.
Holy Mary, Mother of God,
pray for us sinners,
now and at the hour
 of our death. Amen.

Hosanna

HOSANNA

Reproducible Section

New Life Butterfly

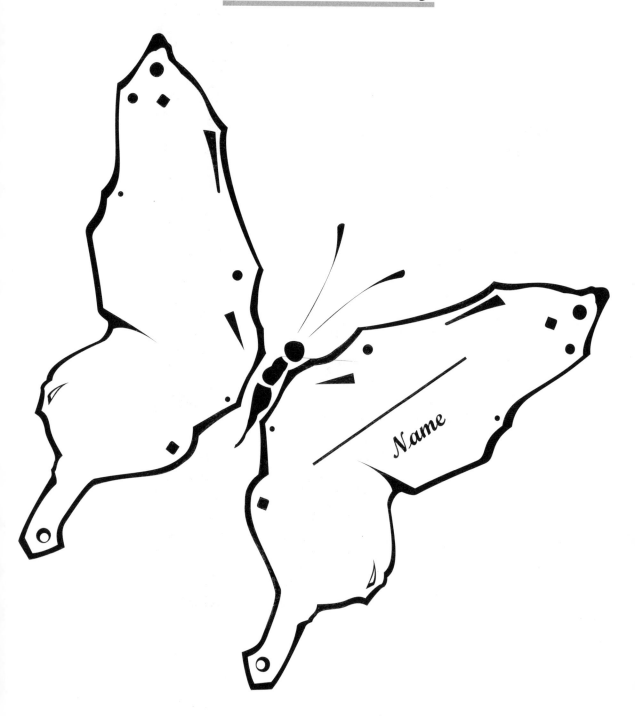

Name

Easter People Pledge

Easter People Pledge

**As a person who has new life
in Jesus Christ, I will do the following
to make the world a better place:**

_____

_____

_____

Signed, _____

I am the way and the truth and the Life (John 14:6)

Easter People Pledge

**As a person who has new life
in Jesus Christ, I will do the following
to make the world a better place:**

_____

_____

_____

Signed, _____

I am the way and the truth and the Life (John 14:6)

Meal Tickets

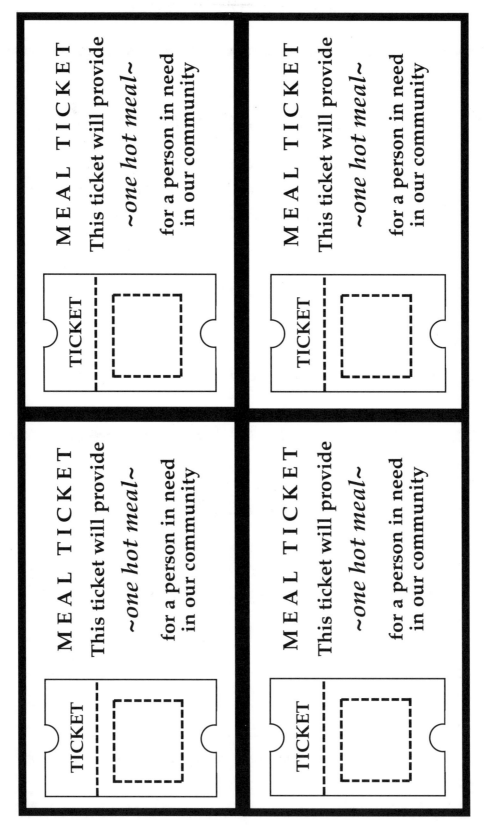

MEAL TICKET

This ticket will provide

~one hot meal~

for a person in need
in our community

TICKET

MEAL TICKET

This ticket will provide

~one hot meal~

for a person in need
in our community

TICKET

MEAL TICKET

This ticket will provide

~one hot meal~

for a person in need
in our community

TICKET

MEAL TICKET

This ticket will provide

~one hot meal~

for a person in need
in our community

TICKET

**I will follow Jesus,
the Good Shepherd.**

_____

(Name)

**I will follow Jesus,
the Good Shepherd.**

_____

(Name)

Reproducible Section

The Apostle's Creed

Read by: _____

We believe in God, the Father Almighty,
Creator of heaven and earth.

Read by: _____

We believe in Jesus Christ, his only Son,
our Lord,
Who was conceived by the Holy Spirit
And born of the Virgin Mary.

Read by: _____

He suffered under Pontius Pilate,
Was crucified, died and was buried.
He descended to the dead and
On the third day he rose again.

Read by: _____

He ascended into heaven,
And is seated at the right hand
of the Father.
He will come again to judge
The living and the dead.

Read by: _____
(Could be divided into 2 parts)

We believe in the Holy Spirit,
The holy catholic Church,
The communion of saints,
The forgiveness of sins,
The resurrection of the body,
And life everlasting.

All say:

Amen.